Lifting the Fire Hydrant Lid

Kate Fullen

JACARANDA

First published in Great Britain 2020 by
Jacaranda Books Art Music Ltd
27 Old Gloucester Street,
London WC1N 3AX
www.jacarandabooksartmusic.co.uk

A CIP catalogue record for this book is available from the
British Library

ISBN: 9781909762947
eISBN: 9781913090036

Cover Design: Christina Schweighardt
Typeset by Kamillah Brandes
Printed and bound by CPI Group (UK) Ltd, Croydon, CR0 4YY

Foreword

This book holds a mirror to the Fire and Rescue Service we are working hard to leave behind.

The journey is not yet complete and there is still much work to be done. But there is now an irreversible momentum to ensure the Fire and Rescue Service becomes the open, inclusive, and progressive Service my colleagues and our communities deserve.

This story is not a comfortable read for those of us who have committed our working lives to the Fire and Rescue Service, but it's a story which needs to be told.

Chris Lowther
Chief Fire Officer
Tyne and Wear Fire and Rescue Service

For Shay and Leon

One

"It takes four seconds to decide if you are going to like someone. In this case, I've decided that I'm going to like you. I don't like small talk so please don't make any.

This is the first and last cup of tea I am ever going to make you."

With that Adam put my tea down and walked out the room.

I stood alone in the station canteen, consumed in stainless steel. The blood red floor had been freshly mopped and the surfaces were bare and polished. The once white, vertical blinds softly announced the cold night air and I hugged my tea. I closed my eyes, inhaled my surroundings and smiled.

That was my Gaffer. The man I would have to entrust with my life and my career.

The first summertime of the millennium was drawing to its official close when I reported to my assigned fire station to meet my new colleagues. Despite my Gaffer's questionably welcoming speech, I felt at home. I had found a purpose and regained an identity. It was a euphoric culmination of a journey that had spanned nearly two decades.

*

On the face of it, my parents were an unlikely couple, as far removed from each other as it was possible to be—my mum was training to be a nun, while my dad attended Woodcote Hall Seminary with the intention of entering the priesthood. I don't know what caused them to defer from their paths, but thankfully, they each discovered a new calling in the teaching profession. They met at University and married in 1971.

I was born in September 1976—the country's hottest summer fizzled out as thunderstorms brought an end to the great drought. It was 14:50 on a Friday afternoon and my dad missed the momentous occasion of my birth as he had raced to the bank to make the 15:00 weekend closing.

Eighteen months earlier my elder brother, Dominic, had been a breech birth and was the first to be delivered in the town's new special baby unit. In many ways, our arrivals typified our personalities—Dom would blaze ahead, causing havoc and attracting attention, whereas I was comfortable in his shadow, understated yet assured.

We lived on a cul-de-sac in Bishop Auckland, a bustling market town in County Durham in the North East of England. It was a close-knit community—every neighbour was a friend and every adult an honorary aunt or uncle. Dom was my best friend, I looked up to him and constantly pushed myself to keep up. Shortly after my third birthday, my younger brother Bernard was born, followed two years later by my sister, Elizabeth. I loved mothering my younger siblings, but I craved adventure and exploration so I continued to spend most of my time attached to Dom's hip. I saw myself as a peer of Dominic and his friends. I climbed the same trees, rode my bike along the same paths and engaged in the same games. We were young and too busy having fun to concern ourselves with gender differences or age hierarchy.

My mum was always around—she ran a happy, comfortable home that had a constant aroma of delicious home-cooked meals. When my dad was not working as a deputy head teacher, he would be on call as a retained fireman, slipping away in the dead of night to race to the station. While he fought fires, my mum would anxiously wait for his return. As children, oblivious to our parents' sleepless nights, we revelled in the simple delights of making dens and fishing with nets and jam jars. With six mouths to feed money was tight, but my parents had a strong work ethic and we did not want for anything. Through my eyes it was the perfect childhood. It was a joyful and carefree time, but everything changed shortly after my 7th birthday.

My dad secured his first Head Teacher post in East Grinstead, West Sussex and we relocated as a family. I travelled with my mum and younger siblings on the train, while Dom and my dad made the day long journey in the car. I was excited about the train, seeing my new house and meeting new people. I did not consider the reality of the days that ensued and I had not fully comprehended that in these circumstances new replaced old.

It was January when I started my second primary school. The playgrounds were allotted to different year groups and I was isolated from my brothers. It was my first real experience of being alone.

A bell rang, and I made my way towards the building.

"You must be the new girl."

An older girl appeared at my shoulder, her face framed by her fleecy hood. I did not like the idea that I must be someone, but I was lost and her guidance was welcome.

"Your class is here."

I took my place in the line, but was pulled out by my teacher who conducted a tour and an information brief on the daily workings of the school. While it was a friendly and necessary introduction, it was also an unwelcome exhibition of my stranger status.

My classmates were a wave of smiling faces and questions rained down on me, but we spoke a different language. My accent forged in the mining towns of the north east was comical to my new contemporaries. In contrast, I associated their dialect with wealth and superiority.

We were seated in groups of six. An equal mix of girls and boys toiled at steely grey rectangular tables and I was grateful for the mathematics problems that distracted my company. I did not enjoy the subject, but the familiarity provided a safe haven and I welcomed it. It was late morning before I summoned the courage to ask a question.

"I'm clamming. What time is bait?"

Glances fired across the table. There were shrugs, raised eyebrows, puzzled faces and barely suppressed amusement. Leaning in, a girl who had told me her name three times, spoke for the group.

"Sorry, but you talk very fast. Could you say that again?"

"Ah, right. Sorry. What time do you have your bait?"

"What time do we what?"

"What time is dinner?"

"Do you mean lunch?"

Every conversation was an effort and I didn't want to be different. I was more comfortable in the background.

I was no stranger to fitting in—I had emulated my older brother and his friends for years. So, that afternoon, I studied my peers and took my lead from them. Over the next few days, I learned to use the full version of every word and avoided phrases that would accentuate my accent. I linked arms with the other girls as we walked aimlessly around the playground. I even attempted to skip. By the end of that first week, I was an image of what I thought was expected.

Outside of school, I played football with Dom and a group of local boys. I was already beginning to settle in this new town.

My family and I spent three eventful years in Sussex. We moved to Ashdown Forest when I was 9 and I had the freedom to explore the woods, join in with marathon football games and roam as I pleased. I believe my love of the outdoors stems from this time as it created a sense of unbelievable freedom and endless adventure.

However, it was also a time when I began to recognise inconsistencies and disparities between my peers and I. The boys were able to play football for a team, but I had to watch from the sidelines. Dom served on the altar at church, but I was told that girls were not allowed. I never felt inferior, but I was driven by the injustice and incongruence. I desperately wanted to play for a team, so I trained harder until some of the lads started asking on my behalf, but the coaches all hid behind rule books, the supposed risk of injuries and the infuriating defence that it was in my best interest.

The church was different. I had no desire to be an altar server, dress in a white robe and stand in front of a congregation, until I was told I couldn't. I had attended church weekly since the day I was born. I loved the idea of miracles and was enchanted by The Parable of the Talents, but the messages of love, support, helping each other and treating everyone the same, were drowned out by the church's notion that I was not equal to my brother. While it was difficult to retain my own sense of worth in the face of such blatant inequality from an established institution, I am grateful that I prevailed.

I had just begun my final year at primary school when Michael Fish famously said,

"Earlier on today, apparently, a woman rung the BBC and said she heard there was a hurricane on the way... well, if you're watching, don't worry, there isn't!"

Hours later the great storm of 1987 hit. Eighteen people lost their lives. A fallen tree missed our house by inches and I was made very aware of the minuscule margins between life and death. Power lines were down, the roads were littered with trees and debris, buildings were damaged. Schools were closed while the wreckage was assessed and transport routes were reopened. My dad made the journey on foot to gauge the damage at the school. He was no stranger to adversity.

A year before the storm, a fire devastated our school. It had just celebrated its centenary and the old building offered no resistance to its obliteration. The fire had annihilated an entire block which had housed two classrooms, the staff room and the offices, but it was no match for the spirit of the staff, pupils, governors and local community. An amazing co-operative effort meant the school reopened after just three days.

I perversely found strength from these natural disasters. I loved how the community were united by a common goal. The fire and the storm had each provided a purpose and a drive to everyone, followed by a tangible sense of achievement and worth. It was intoxicating.

Two months after the storm we moved again. My dad obtained a headship in Harrogate and my parents bought a house in Glasshouses, a beautiful picturesque settlement in the heart of the Yorkshire Dales. It was another adventure, a new place to explore. I had made friends in our old town, but I was by now accustomed to transience.

Our move north was primarily fuelled by a desire to be closer to our extended family. My paternal grandparents lived in Lanchester and we had made the 30-minute drive regularly from Bishop Auckland. Tragically, the night before I was due to start my third school, Grandad died in his sleep. My world had once again turned upside down.

My grandad was a quiet, unassuming man. He would sit in his corner chair next to the electric fire, smoke his pipe and watch as the frenzied activity of his grandchildren and his hospitable wife unfolded in front of him. The room would still the instant he spoke—we hung on his every word. Grandad was a man of few words, but his actions spoke volumes. He took my siblings and me on trips to the river and would carve us swords on demand. I took time for granted and he died without me ever really getting to know the man behind the fun. He had kept a great deal of his life private and even my grandma was astounded by the volume of people who contacted her in the days and weeks following his death to explain how her husband had helped them.

We spent several days at my grandma's house along with aunties, uncles and cousins. My grandad had left a huge void, but it was comforting to be amongst family. After the funeral, we returned to Yorkshire, our home of just two weeks, and I started school a week later than planned.

Things were looking down. My dad had lost his father and had a new school to lead. Dom was alone at secondary school, Bernard was seven and Liz had just started reception. My Mum had a home to run and a family to care for in an alien environment. At eleven years old, I lacked the emotional maturity to recognise my own needs. I did not want to add to my family's suffering and I did not want to discuss my feelings of loss with people I had not yet met. I created a strong public persona, primarily as a means of coping. I broke out from the comfortable obscurity of a crowd and learned to think and act for myself.

I was sitting at a table amongst my newest classmates when a pretty girl with long blonde hair delivered her verdict:

"You aren't like we imagined."

It was a strange feeling, that of being imagined, and the use of the plural told me I had also been discussed. My interest was piqued.

"What did you imagine?"

The pretty girl now had a crimson face.

"Well, you know." She paused and tried to return to her essay, hoping that was enough, but the silence encouraged her to continue.

"We thought..." the others all became absorbed in their work. I began to feel uneasy.

"We thought you would be, you know, like a proper Headmaster's daughter..."

I recognised that feeling in my stomach. I was four years old when a size 5 football had hit me square in my mid-drift, momentarily emptying my lungs from the unexpected impact.

I looked around at the faces. Their smiles suggested it was a compliment, but I was winded. I was Kate. I had created several versions of myself, but I was me. I had no idea that I could be seen as an extension of someone else and now I was acutely aware that, to some people, I was simply my father's daughter. I wanted to be known in my own right, for who I was. I was the sum of my own successes and failures, not anyone else's.

"…blond, quite small and posh."

"No," I was deflated. "I'm just me."

The conversation continued around me and it was decided that I was down to earth and normal. I had achieved acceptance, but I had paid with my identity. New starts had followed a similar pattern. Initial exchanges were brief as a class competed to be heard. Questions were fired and I replied at speed. I presented the best version of myself and people saw what they wanted to see.

I was drained and emotional. I lacked the energy to deal with excited chatter and incessant questions. I craved some peace, some distance from the crowd, but I was torn. I still wanted to be liked and I didn't want to be seen as unfriendly.

I was grateful for my packed lunch. The majority of my class had school dinners and a handful of us sat in a classroom. That was when I noticed Alexis. While other children were seeking out companionship, comparing their respective lunches and swapping wares, one girl sat apart. She was considerably smaller than me, with a slight frame and cropped hair the colour of wet sand.

The image conjured memories of my Grandad sitting in his chair and I swallowed before the lump could take hold in my throat. Alexis had an aura of calmness and peace. She seemed unconcerned with the rest of the world, but content with her place in it. I had been so absorbed in my own thoughts, I only just realised she was clothed differently.

While every other child was dressed in regulatory grey jumpers, Alexis was wrapped in a blue cardigan. I studied her for several minutes as she worked her way methodically through her lunch and grew increasingly intrigued.

Eventually I sidled over.

"Hi."

Alexis closed her lunch box, looked up and smiled warmly.

"Hi."

That was it. No questions as to my name, background or new girl status. I was pleased, but slightly thrown by her indifference.

"Why are you wearing that blue cardigan?"

"It's cold."

"But it's blue."

"I know."

"Why are you not wearing a grey one?"

Alexis looked straight at me, her eyes scrunched in confusion. "Because I don't have a grey cardigan."

"Have you got a grey jumper?" I had not enjoyed my experience of being different and I was concerned for her.

"Yes."

"Why don't you wear that?"

"Because this is warmer." She smiled as she stood up.

The school lunch diners were pouring onto the yard. Alexis made to join them and I followed her. We quickly became friends and partnered up for the weekly class trip to the swimming baths. Alexis' Mum would come along too, walking behind with our class teacher. While many of us now found our parents embarrassing, Alexis would simply joke that her Mum had a thing for Mr. McNally.

Life appeared straightforward for Alexis. I was in awe of her as she effortlessly combined her affable nature with a bold expression of individuality. I secretly envied her inner strength and confidence to be herself.

Nine months later we started secondary school together at St. John Fisher's High School, but we were placed in different classes.

It was a 15-mile journey and I had left home at 07:15, walked to the top of the village and caught the 07:30 school bus. I was welcomed by my new teachers to the tune of, "If you are anything like your brother, we are not going to get on."

Fortunately, I did get on with most of my teachers. I was naturally strategic and logical—I had won three consecutive national chess titles by the time I was nine and I understood how to make my school life work for me. I found the classrooms distracting and struggled to focus on the subject matter, so I would learn the material myself in the evenings.

The work was manageable and I coped without excelling in most areas. I didn't mind the effort—it was a means to an end. I recognised that I needed to keep my parents and teachers happy to maximise the time I could spend playing football and hanging around with my friends.

My secondary school life revolved around sport and my lunchtimes became consumed by team practices. My friendships were forged from the activities I took part in, whereas Alexis' interests lay elsewhere, primarily in business. Consequently, we rarely spent time together. However, we enjoyed a shared sense of humour and an alliance that was based on familiarity and fun. She remained a reassuring constant in my life and I enjoyed the security, comfort and fluency of a history shared. Our paths ran alongside each other, rarely touching but always close by. I was delighted when we each chose to attend the University of Sunderland.

I was weeks away from starting university life and enjoying the last remnants of summer when I answered the phone in my Dad's study. It was Maureen, a teacher at my Father's school. He was out and I agreed to take a message.

"Will you tell him that Alexis Taylor died last night?"

My breath lodged in my throat. I sank into the chair and stared at the window. It looked out onto the main road running through the village and framed an oak tree. Its burnt yellow and sun-drenched orange leaves littered the dry-stone wall that homed our front garden. I had been standing in that very scene five minutes earlier, laughing with friends.

My mind reacted to the shockwave of Alexis' death by creating a happier picture. I could see my friends chatting animatedly, catching sight of me at the window, they beam and wave. I closed my eyes and took a deep breath. When I opened them, only the background remained.

Maureen continued, "I'm so sorry Kate; she was in your year, wasn't she?"

"I'll tell my Dad." I didn't want to sound curt, but I could barely speak. I needed to end the conversation.

I had known Alexis since I was eleven years old. She had been born with cystic fibrosis and with a hole in her heart. But I only found this out at her funeral. Alexis did not mention it and I never considered that our plans to attend university together would not come about.

I thought back on the previous few months and felt increasingly nauseous. All the signs had been there; she had become increasingly frail and needed to be carried up the stairs to lessons. There had been practice fire alarms and Alexis had been excused from leaving the building. It was evident that she was ill, but I assumed she would recover during the holidays. Between exams and revision and the fact we could all now legally drink, it was far from surprising that she was run down. It never once occurred to me that she was dying.

In the immediate aftermath of Alexis' death, I was numb. Nothing made sense. The image of her working hard, investing in a future that never materialized, tormented me and I deeply regretted that I never got to say a proper goodbye.

Alexis and I did not share friendship groups. It only became apparent to me when I had no-one to share my memories with. I decided to write to Gabs, Alexis' mum.

Two weeks after Alexis' funeral, I started at Sunderland University. A letter was waiting for me. It was from Gabs and two lines in particular have always stayed with me:

"Make something of your life, my love. Show life what you are made of."

I saw myself as the second athlete of a relay team; Alexis had run her leg with humour, confidence, humility, enthusiasm and endeavour. I took the baton, but spent the next several years running in the wrong direction.

Two

I began my Sport Science degree in the autumn of 1995. However, my studies soon became secondary to drinking, playing football and socializing.

I didn't know what I wanted. My goal was simply to experience as many things as possible.

During this time, I lost other friends. One of the lads I played football with was killed during a bike race, whilst anorexia claimed the life of a school friend. I developed a fear of regret and missing out so I said yes to everything.

I applied for a job as a Lifeguard at a swimming pool in Sunderland. I had previous experience working in Harrogate whilst I had completed my A levels and passed the necessary tests. The interview was winding up when I was asked,

"Can you skate?"

The question was not altogether unrelated as there was an ice rink in the centre.

"Err yeah."

"Great, the skating assessment will take place after

lunch."

I laughed.

He didn't.

Technically it wasn't a lie. Although I had never tried to skate, I had no reason to believe I couldn't do it. Lacing my boots, I got a last-minute tip from one of the other candidates,

"When it comes to picking up the penny, give it a little kick first."

"Great, thanks."

As it turned out, I didn't need to worry about the penny, nor the chicane of cones. My inability to skate was painfully apparent from the moment we were told to warm up. As the rest of the group floated gracefully across the ice, I crashed from barrier to barrier, the tell-tale sound reverberating across the empty rink.

I was on the floor, midway through my sixth attempt to stand up when an instructor glided over. He offered a hand, which I gratefully accepted.

"Don't worry about it. You can hand the skates out and change the music."

Result.

University provided my first opportunity to play football for a team and I loved the sense of belonging. Outside of lectures we did everything together and much of our socialising took place in the student bar. My life was transient and I lived for the moment. I enjoyed the company of friends, but I struggled to form meaningful relationships as I didn't expect anything to last. Some friends dropped out, others moved to different universities or graduated and moved on. I missed my school mates, we had been a tight bunch, especially throughout sixth form, and starting all over again was hard. I was grateful that one friend, Claire, joined me at university. She was a great laugh, a confidante and a reassuring anchor. However, while Claire grew as a person, organised herself and balanced her immediate needs with those of her future, I was painfully aware of the fragility of life and vowed to enjoy what time I had. I completed all the necessary work, but I never pushed myself to discover what I was actually capable of. Consequently, I graduated three years later in 1998, with a second-class honours.

I loved seeing the pride in my family's faces when they attended my graduation ceremony and I enjoyed the excitement of new beginnings, but I did not relish the transition into the world of work and responsibilities. I delayed the inevitable and spent the summer watching the world cup in Paris with some fellow graduates, before working full time at the University of Newcastle as a sports hall attendant.

I was also homeless. An agreement with my housemates to continue living together was flawed when I became the only one to secure employment in the North East.

As the others, Claire included, returned to their families, I was grateful for some floor space in my friend's room. I had left it too late to find alternative flat mates and my wages would not stretch to cover the rent on my own place.

I met Sophie playing for the University football team. We shared similar interests and were often the last ones remaining in the pub. She was a few years older and was now working as a housing officer at Newcastle University. It was necessity that first drove us together, but we soon became almost constant companions.

I loved life. I had a brilliant social network with younger university friends who were still students, Sophie was the perfect collaborator for my many schemes and my new colleagues were fantastic company. The only cloud in my eternal blue sky was my boss.

My manager was an ex-professional footballer. He had an excellent scoring record for the staff 5 a side football team, but little experience of women in the work environment. I had only been in my new employment for three weeks when I was summoned to speak with him.

Colin reminded me of a mole, constantly holed up in his office. He was taller than me, but his quiet demeanour and ability to seemingly shrink into himself made him appear smaller. He struggled to maintain eye contact and was driven by nervous energy.

"Sit down, sit down."

I took a seat opposite him across the desk.

"So, how are you settling in? Everything ok?" Colin was sitting with his hands together, fingertips touching, his elbows resting on the arms of the chair. He was a visual representation of interest.

"Yes thanks, everyone has been really welcoming."

"Good." Colin nodded.

I nodded too. Partly because I agreed that everyone being welcoming was good, but also because I got the impression he was going somewhere and I didn't want him to get sidelined by anything I had to say.

"Everything ok at home?" Colin placed both his index fingers on the table, shoulder width apart.

"Yeah."

"You live with Sophie, right?" At this point he slid his two index fingers across the desk and started bouncing them together.

"Not like that!" I nodded towards his fingers, incredulous.

Across the desk, this middle aged, balding gentleman with an unblemished career hastily removed his fingers from the desk.

"I didn't mean like that! I just wanted to make sure you were alright!"

"Well, I am thanks. Everything is fine. Work is fine and my housemate Sophie is fine."

"Good."

"Was that everything?"

"Yes, that was all thanks."

I went back downstairs and was only halfway through recounting the story to the receptionist, when my flustered manager arrived, briefcase in hand, and announced that he would be out for the remainder of the day.

On reflection, I felt a pang of guilt. I had overreacted and taken offence at a seemingly innocent question. My sexuality was inconsequential to me. I didn't identify with either gay or straight. I didn't like labels nor the requirement to assign a person to a specific box, which is generally governed by preconceptions. Who I chose to sleep with didn't define who I was and had no influence on my ability to do my job, and while I was happy to discuss my private life, it infuriated me when it was done in an official capacity. I'll never know my manager's motivation for his line of questioning, but there's every chance that he was a decent, kind man with unfortunate hand gestures.

My job was not taxing. I had to assemble 5 a side goals, badminton nets and release the basketball hoops in line with the activity timetable.

I began the role with the enthusiasm and endeavour that is often associated with new ventures, but I became increasingly agitated at the mundane nature of my employment. I endured three consecutive monthly meetings that contained only one item on the agenda. Each month we would convene in the meeting room. A conference table filled the area, polished and hoovered according to the weekly cleaning schedule, it had the aura of a seldom used room. As a dozen people took their seats, the air circulated and the chamber grudgingly came to life. Colin opened up the meeting.

"Welcome everyone. Thank you for coming. We will

crack straight onto the first item on the agenda. Which is…"

Colin looked down at his notes.

"…John is still not wearing his radio."

He turned to a silver haired man, tall and thin, his face littered with the distinctive lines of a heavy smoker. He was also a sports hall attendant, but we covered different shifts.

"John, will you be wearing the radio from now on?"

"No."

"Ok, I'll put that down to be discussed at the next meeting." There was a brief pause while Colin made notes.

"Moving on to item number two. Any other business?"

The first two meetings I attended were duplicates of each other. John was unable to attend the third meeting due to union commitments so the matter was postponed until, "John can update us properly."

It was rare that anyone had any other business, but on occasion it was deemed necessary to check that everyone was happy with the selection of biscuits in the staff room.

My day to day activities were not much better. Colin would come racing down from his office if he could see that I was moving some equipment and insist that he at least took half of it.

"It's fine Colin, I've got this." I was dragging the equipment away from him in a desperate attempt to keep it from his reach.

He was running after me, arms outstretched.

"No Kate, these posts are heavy."

"It's ok, I manage fine on evenings and weekends when I'm here by myself!"

Colin missed the point and I limited my frustrations to seething and glares, until I met Sophie in the pub at lunch.

"It's so annoying! He won't let me do anything. And it's embarrassing. Everyone stares while two of us set up a badminton net. Those things are on wheels. I don't even have to lift them!"

Sophie listened as she tucked into her jacket potato. Officially, we only had 30 minutes for lunch. Walking and waiting for the food to arrive did not allow much time to eat. As the badminton court was booked for an hour and my boss did most of my work, I didn't share my friend's urgency.

Sophie paused to take a drink.

"Why don't you talk to him?"

"I've tried. Several times."

Sophie had gone back to eating so I continued,

"And, I can't even show him. I'm literally running out with the equipment to try and get it out before he gets there. I carried the 5 a side goal the width of the hall and he grabbed it with a metre to go and said, 'There you go!'"

Sophie looked up and smiled, she didn't need to contribute now I was on a roll.

"And, another thing, did I tell you about the picture?"

"No, tell me about the picture."

She had finished her meal and was leaning back, drink in hand, ready for the full story.

"He came in the other day and asked me to put a picture

up."

"Right, well that's good if he's asking you to do something."

"Yeah, but then he tells me he'll show me where the hammer is. So, I follow him upstairs. We both go to the drawer with the hammer inside. Colin takes it out and says, 'Next, we get the nails.'"

Sophie snorted out her drink, "I see why he's a manager."

"It gets worse, mate. We both go to the cupboard with the nails in, so now Colin has the nails in one hand and his hammer in the other. Then he says he would show me where he wants it, but first we have to go back to his office to get the picture."

I was getting more animated while my best friend pursed her lips, her eyes bulging from the effort of holding in her laugh.

"He has his hands full with the hammer and nails so he lets me hold the picture and we go downstairs. And then he says, 'So, if you just put the nail in like this,' as he's banging the nail into the wall, 'and hang the picture, like this…' And he grabs the picture off me!"

I can suddenly see the funny side and laughter punctuates my finale.

"'Perfect,' he says! Thanks very much!"

It was beyond frustrating. I had desperately wanted to demonstrate my proficiency, but Colin insisted on holding my hand throughout my employment. The leash was so short I could neither impress nor disappoint.

Ultimately, I gave up. I wanted a sense of control over the situation, so I would amuse the receptionists by seeing exactly what I could get him to do. He once showed me exactly how to clean a cupboard.

Three

I was twenty-two when Manchester United secured the Treble in May 1999 and I had created the life I wanted. Sophie had used her contacts to secure a house at a reasonable rate in the west end of Newcastle. The confines of a shared room, coupled with a joint daily commute, placed a huge strain on our friendship and the move to a three-bedroom house, complete with garden and garage was a welcome one. In addition to the extra living area, it was within cycling distance to the university and a short bus ride to Newcastle City Centre and its notorious nightlife. I was living with my best friend, an ever-obliging drinking and socializing partner. I could do my job with a hangover. I laughed every day with my colleagues, and I had free gym membership. I was living the life of a student, without the deadlines and with money in my pocket. The problem was, I was becoming comfortably numb.

As the 20th century drew to a close, I began to understand why Alexis had committed so much of her time to studying. She had invested that time in herself, giving herself the best possible life by experiencing every part of it—hardships, friendships, triumphs and falls. In contrast, I had devoted my life to having a laugh, and whilst it was enjoyable and effortless, it soon became bland. Nights out followed a familiar path and I saw the same faces, in the same bars, at the same times. My work didn't offer any further sense of fulfilment. Gab's words were never far from my thoughts and I knew I had to initiate a change. I handed my notice to Colin and left work one week later.

I longed to go back home, sit down to a delicious home cooked meal surrounded by my family, but I resisted the temptation. Familiarity would have been comforting, but it had been four years since I had lived at home. I had become accustomed to freedom and independence. I had to move forward.

I spent the following day at the library and applied for any sports related job worldwide. Despite casting a huge net, I landed a job as a swimming pool manager at a local secondary school. It was different and I was given more responsibility, but it was a short-term fix, something else to put on my CV. I was still researching job opportunities and dissecting the Newcastle Evening Chronicle's 'Situations Vacant' pages on a Thursday night when I saw an opportunity on a teletext page covering the local news:

"Open day for Women at Tyne and Wear Fire Brigade"

I leaned forwards, my elbows resting on my knees as I keyed in the numbers of the teletext page on the remote.

"Ever thought about becoming a firefighter? Come

along to our open day tonight and find out more."

This was it. This was exactly what I wanted to do. I couldn't believe I hadn't thought of it before. My Dad had been a retained firefighter while we lived in County Durham; he juggled it with a deputy headship and had to leave it behind when we relocated to Sussex. His fire station was opposite a swimming pool, where Dom and I trained three evenings a week. We would sometimes go to the Fire Station club afterwards for crisps and pop. Even at that young age, I remember feeling a sense that we were welcome and that we belonged there.

The problem with the open day was that I could not drive and, as the event was not public transport friendly, I had to sell it to Sophie. I was off work so I rang her excitedly, tumbling over my words. I held my breath while I waited for her response.

"Well, rugby training's cancelled, so yeah I can take you."

We drove to the event in almost complete silence, but as we got closer, Sophie began an intense line of questioning.

"What will we have to do?"

"I don't know, mate."

"Well, will there be loads of people?"

"I don't know"

"Will they ask us what we know about the fire brigade?"

"I hope not."

"Do we have to do any tests?"

"I'm not sure."

"Are you sure this is the right place?"

"I don't know, mate, honestly. I have no idea. I only read about it on teletext and I told you exactly what it said. You know as much as I do!"

When I woke up that morning, firefighting was not even on the periphery of my orbit of thoughts, but after chancing on that page, I had spent the day fantasizing about being a firefighter. It had consumed me and it was expeditiously the one thing that mattered. Sophie's questions betrayed her nonchalant demeanour. We were both experiencing the enchanting feeling that our lives could be about to change.

The evening was a whirlwind and I was fully caught up in it. The event was exclusively for women, designed to show a window into the world of firefighting. I was invested in the process from the very beginning. I didn't need further information. I only wanted to know if it was possible. A score of us assembled in what looked like a classroom. There were two instructors, one perched on the edge of a table, while the other stood to his side. My eyes were drawn to the device that lay on the table between them.

The standing man spoke first.

"Ok, ladies. This is the grip test. It's designed to assess the strength of the hand and forearm muscles, which is a good indicator of overall strength."

The sitting man then said,

"It's the test we find most women fail on."

His words punched me in my stomach.

I had never done a test like this before and I cursed my

haphazard attendance throughout my degree. I had no point of reference as to my physical strength. That device could put an end to my newly found dream job.

"Does anyone want a turn?"

I raised my hand and the sitting instructor handed me the device. At a time when you could play snake on your mobile phone, the device seemed antiquated. It was about the size and weight of a paperback book. There was a hollow metal square at the bottom with a semi-circle scale on the top. The bottom of the contraption was to sit on my palm and I was shown how a small dial adjusted a bar that ran midway across the square to allow the tips of my fingers to curl around it.

"Hold it above your head with a straight arm"

I followed the instructions.

"Keep your arm straight and grip your hand together into a fist, bring your arm out to the side and down. Keep squeezing, until your hand is by your hip."

I nodded at him.

I took a deep breath. This was it. I channelled every thought and every effort into pressing that bar down. My knuckles were white, every ligament in my hand visible. As my hand rested at the hip, the last drip of effort was wrung out.

The instructor took the device from me and I held my breath.

"Well done. That would be a pass."

I floated through the rest of the evening; I had what I

came for.

Sophie and I walked in silence back to the car.

Shutting my passenger side door, I got my question in first.

"What did you think?"

"Yeah, it was good. Are you going to apply?"

"Too right I am. Are you?"

"Yeah." There was a pause. "Do you think we can do it?"

We sat in the darkness looking at the building that had moulded our common goal. In this moment, it was all possible. We had both passed the tests we were shown, but we were independently harbouring the kind of self-doubt that surfaces when a dream is in sight. We were giving ourselves permission to fail—a survival mechanism to protect against extreme disappointment.

I looked across at Sophie as she started the car.

"Sure we can, mate. This time next year we will be firefighters!"

Four

When the recruitment advert was released two weeks later our enthusiasm reached another level. Our application forms arrived along with an explanation about the expected volume of submissions. All we could do was concentrate on one stage at a time and negotiate each obstacle as we came to it. I completed the form with meticulous detail, ensuring I covered every conceivable angle. The recruitment team were looking for examples of when I had worked at height, in confined spaces, in arduous conditions and as a member of a team. I also needed to explain a time when I was able to follow instructions and another when I had taken a leadership role. Every word was painstakingly considered. Sophie and I had very different backgrounds and experience, but our applications were both carved from several days of complete commitment to the task. We used every possible minute and dropped the forms through the letterbox the night before the deadline. Then we waited.

I didn't have to wait long; the letter came through the mail four days later. I made sure I was alone when I removed the letter carefully from its envelope and held my breath. I scanned the contents over quickly but my eyes stuck to one single sentence:

"…We would like to invite you to the next stage."

I clutched the letter to my chest and clenched my fist, silently celebrating as my body created its own version of champagne. Bubbles formed in my stomach until the pressure was released through my mouth.

"YES!"

I sat on my bed and reread the letter, savouring the effervescence.

A week later, I reported to my written exam at the brigade headquarters in the heart of Newcastle along with 60 other hopefuls. I could only see one other woman. My thoughts turned to Sophie and I hoped she would hear from them soon. I was confident as I took a seat amongst the rows of single tables, but my buoyancy took a dive after I turned the page.

The questions focused on situational awareness, problem solving and understanding information. The whole process took an exhausting three hours. I filed out with the others, having used all the available time and answered each question with consideration. There was nothing else I could do.

The next day, Sophie's letter arrived inviting her to the next stage. I was thrilled for her, but I could not help feeling a tinge of jealousy. My friend's application to be a firefighter was definitely alive while my odds were back to 50/50.

"Can you remember any of the questions?"

"Only the ones I told you... "

Sophie looked deflated, so I expanded.

"The questions are all straight-forward, you'll be totally fine."

My confidence was feigned. I had no idea how well I had done so I could not accurately assess my friend's prospects, but we had to believe that we were going to be successful and prepare mentally and physically for subsequent tests. We stepped up our gym visits from three to five times a week and concentrated our efforts on the free weights and resistance machines.

It was two weeks before I heard anything. I handled the envelope with sickening anticipation. I took heart at the thickness of the package—surely it would only require a single sheet of A4 to tell me I had been unsuccessful. I opened the envelope carefully along the seal, and removed the contents. A map floated to the floor and my heart leapt. The additional sheets contained the details of the next phase of the selection process. My dream was still alive. My success also buoyed Sophie and she soon received official confirmation that she was invited to the next stage.

The fitness tests followed, but before we could concentrate on them, Sophie and I had to move home. The house we had occupied had been sold and we relocated to a flat in Wideopen, a suburb which lay three miles north of the city. It was January and the landlord was willing to rent it to us until student tenants took over in September.

The brigade occupational health department was situated at the rear of a fire station in the west of the city. I boarded a bus, made my way upstairs and looked out the window in an attempt to relax.

Thanks to my sports science degree and the open evening at the fire service headquarters, I had prior experience of all the tests. They measured my lung function, heart rate, grip strength and flexibility. I left feeling confident and soon received notification to attend the next stage, but I had a decision to make.

I had received a job offer. White Water Rafting Instructor on Pigeon River, Nashville, Tennessee. It was an amazing opportunity and promised the adventure I was itching for. I was undeniably interested and I agonised over the decision, but the idea of a career, the opportunity to make a difference and the craving for a sense of belonging won out. Passing up on such an incredible experience for the chance of being a firefighter intensified the pressure of making the grade.

Applicants who were successful at the work-related assessment day would be invited to an interview and then only a medical and an eye test remained. It was the stage that most people failed on, and given the diverse range of tests involved I could see why.

The journey to the training centre was a task in itself. It required several changes of buses and I found myself in parts of the north east that I didn't know existed. A taxi took me the rest of the way. It was an expense I could barely afford, but an investment I had to make.

I registered alongside eleven other candidates and we lined up for our first ordeal. The 'bleep test' was a widely-used fitness test and involved running 20-metre shuttles. It was designed to include a warm up and began at a moderate walking speed, increasing steadily in pace. Often the subject would continue until they reached their maximum exertion, but in this case the pass mark was level 9.6 so I had a target. The goal was not particularly high—it was rated 'good' as an indicator of fitness, but I hated running. I loathed cross country at school and generally finished marginally ahead of the heavy smokers. I was not blessed with speed or endurance and I was fortunate that technical ability and commitment masked my shortcomings in team events. I had been told I have the perfect figure for Ice Climbing, but I had yet to test that theory.

Standing on the starting line, I had no doubt that I would complete this task. I knew where I had to get and I would force myself through any barrier to get there. As we approached level 9.6, I was relieved and silently congratulated myself, unfortunately however, no-one stopped. We continued to level 10 and then followed an instructor on a few laps of the yard. I was exhausted and breathing hard. I had exceeded my perceived limits several minutes ago; it was a bitter morning and my lungs were raw. I felt like I was inhaling shards of glass. I focused solely on the trainers of the person in front. Their owners had an effortless running style, bouncing on their toes in a seemingly self-propelling motion. In contrast, the yard absorbed every ounce of energy of my feet pounding the ground.

I knew this discomfort would pass the instant I ceased running, but if I stopped prematurely, the regret would last forever. Whatever it took, I would not stop. Nobody did.

I had never been so happy to see a lecture room. The fire-fighter recruit course requires a great deal of information to be processed and a huge amount of physical work. To demonstrate that we could retain new material while fatigued, we were to sit through a lecture and be tested on the content. My mind had a tendency to wander. I struggled to keep up with lessons at sixth form and would digest the information on my own away from the classroom. I did not have that option here. I had to let go of my ecstatic thoughts of the bleep test, along with concerns over the rest of the day, and concentrate on the present.

The hose run was next. There was only one way to practise this test and that was to go to a fire station and do it. I had tried it on several occasions, and at more than one station in case I had pushed the boundaries of the fire-fighters' patience. I knew I could do it, but there were so many variables, so many things that could go wrong. We were kitted out in full fire kit. Boots that I had never worn before, fire leggings and tunic that were several sizes too big, a helmet that kept slipping down in front of my eyes and gloves that hung an inch over my fingers.

We had to run out a coiled length of hose and roll it

back up again six times, and we were given eight minutes to do it. As I rolled my length of hose over the line for the sixth time, my thighs were burning, I was drenched in sweat and my heart was racing, but I had finished with minutes to spare and was buzzing with confidence and anticipation.

We were then given sixty seconds to climb the 13.5 metre ladder, hook a leg through a round and lean back. I was comfortable with heights but struggled to get my over-sized boot through a round, and I entered the final assessment concerned that I had not made the time.

Waiting in a holding area for the confined space trial, I had an opportunity to speak to some of my fellow candidates.

"I've done this before," one of them said.

My eyes instinctively widened as I looked at him. His sweat soaked t-shirt clung to his chiselled chest and his biceps bulged as his hand rested casually against the wall. This guy was a sure thing. I couldn't imagine him failing at anything.

I leaned forward, eager for any forthcoming information, when another lad spoke.

"Yeah, me too."

I was a meerkat watching a tennis match.

"And me."

I settled back as the conversation played out in front of me.

"I failed on my eye test, so I had them lasered."

I admired his dedication and was envious of his justified

confidence in success this time round, but that was short lived.

"I passed everything."

"Me too."

I looked to the ceiling and waited for their version of how fate had conspired against them, but the laser eye guy spoke.

"It's a nightmare, isn't it? My mate's passed everything three times, but can't get through the random selection."

"What?" I involved myself. "So, passing all of the tests doesn't guarantee you a job?"

There were ten of us in that small space, and six pairs of eyes followed my question. Our three wise men shook their heads.

"No, there are always loads more people that pass than places on the course, so the final selection is a lottery."

I was crushed. I had assumed my fate would have been in my own hands. Now, all I could do was make sure I had a ticket for the draw.

When the time arrived, the thickness of the parcel offered no comfort as I deduced that it could have indicated the extent of my failings. I turned it over in my hand, trying to see if I could make out a keyword. I felt sick and lightheaded. I put the envelope down and considered the worst-case scenario. It was not that bad. Nothing would change. I had experience of the tests and firefighting was a possible career option even if it was a few years down the line. I downplayed the importance of the contents as much as possible and gained the necessary courage to read the letter. I held my breath and my heart raced, my mouth was dry and my hands were shaking. I tried to start at the top, but my eyes were immediately drawn to the part that mattered:

'We would like to… invite you to an interview.'

I had done it!

I was ecstatic and after I jumped around the empty flat and reread the letter several times, I waited for Sophie to come home.

"Mate, I passed! I've got an interview next week!"

To her credit, Sophie was genuinely pleased for me, but I curbed my celebrations until her letter arrived.

I rang her at work, eager to open the envelope on her behalf, but she insisted on waiting until she got home. I got it. I was exactly the same. I could never understand students who opened exam results together. I needed the time and space to let things sink in before I could share them with others. Sophie did pass and we both were on the final strait. An interview, a medical and an eye test were all that stood between us and a career as firefighters.

I went back to the fire stations who had helped me prepare for the hose run and absorbed every drop of advice they offered. I was comfortable in the interview environment and the ensuing medical and eye test were almost formalities, but I was still susceptible to the apparent random selection.

I didn't mind the wait because the lack of news kept

my goal alive. It was the sight of the letter on my doormat that caused my heart to pound with anticipation. I froze momentarily as my body interpreted signs of a flight or fight response. The situation was not life or death and my breathing slowed accordingly, but my stomach sank, opening a chasm of expectation as my hands fumbled with the envelope. My palms were sweating and I noticed that I was uncomfortably hot. I held my breath as I turned over the solitary sheet of A4. Finally, there it was, written in black and white. I had been successful and was offered a place on the next recruit course in four weeks' time.

I felt like I was four years old, standing at the top of my estate, my heart thumping at the exertion of the climb. I paused for a moment, savouring the expectation. Then I climbed onto my rabbit on wheels and held on for my life. I was in free fall. The exhilaration of adrenalin and adventure was equalled by the comforting knowledge that when the ride ended, I would be home.

Five

Sophie discovered she had also been successful two days later. I was still on an incredible personal high, but sharing the experience elevated my exhilaration and joy to new levels. We were buzzing with excitement and hit the town to celebrate. We apportioned ourselves the time to absorb the moment before sharing our news. To us, it was more than a job offer. It was proof that we could achieve a dream. We had provided the sweat and industry, endured the necessary stress and applied complete commitment to the goal. It had culminated in a success that we owned. I had updated my family periodically throughout the recruitment, but I kept things low key. Personal disappointment would be difficult enough. I did not relish being responsible for anyone else's.

My parents were genuinely pleased that I'd succeeded in landing my dream job, but their joy was slightly curtailed by the acknowledgement that I would be staying in the north east. We were all growing up and leaving home. My mum and dad had a brilliant social life and an extensive network of friends, maintaining contact with both the families on our estate in Bishop Auckland and teachers and parents from our time in East Sussex. They were active members of the church and the local community and negotiated the transition from hectic family home to an empty nest with their trademark relaxed nature. They may have had reservations about my chosen career. My dad had seen the dangers of firefighting first hand and my mum had spent countless hours waiting for him to come home. However, they never voiced their concerns or tried to influence my decision. I am extremely grateful that my parents have always allowed me to make my own choices. Their unwavering support has acted as a safety net throughout my life, giving me the confidence to try new things without a fear of failure.

I worked my four-week notice at the swimming pool and increasingly swapped training sessions for a night on the beer. Sophie and I had several pockets of friends and we celebrated our success with each of them: two groups of work colleagues, her rugby team, my football team, university friends and allies we had met from our regular visits to the pubs. The celebratory drinks then merged into goodbye drinks. We could not afford the risk of picking up an injury and jeopardising our new employment, so we took the decision to quit our respective sports teams for at least the duration of the recruit course. The farewell sessions hit home the fact that our lives would change, initially by the demands of the course and then by the confines of shift work. When we had finished saying goodbye, we were left with excitement for what lay ahead and that was sufficient justification for another trip to the pub. As I approached the training centre for the first time as a new recruit, I instantly regretted my month long drinking session.

My stomach knotted as I set foot inside. The building was sterile and oppressive. White breezeblock walls were sparsely decorated by occasional photographs of official looking gentlemen sporting moustaches, and a matte blue polished floor stretched out before me. The pungent mix of stale sweat and smoke hanging in the air was the solitary indicator of the building's function. This was my first experience of a uniformed, disciplined service and I was out of my depth. I decided my best chance of survival was to keep my head down, do my work and stay under the radar.

I gathered with my fellow recruits in a lecture room, but no-one was sitting. Testosterone filled the room and nobody was prepared to take a seat. There was a buzz of conversation as 24 excited people met for the first time. Sophie and I were stood in close proximity, but we were both involved in different conversations when the incident that would affect my entire time at training school happened.

I felt a nudge in my back and turned to find Sophie manically gesturing towards the front of the room.

"That was you! They just called your name!"

I followed my friend's gaze and saw two large men, one dark and one blonde, both immaculately dressed in uniform and clean shaven. Black ties rested on short sleeved, pale blue shirts. Black epaulettes with two solid silver lines decorated their shoulders, a single red lanyard looped around their left shoulder and a perfect crease ran down each muscular arm. The fair-haired guy held a clipboard while both men's eyes darted around the room.

I looked back at Sophie. "Are you sure?"

"Yes!"

I hesitated. There was no reason for my name to have been read out first. Alphabetically there was bound to have been someone before F, but that hesitation, that slightest pause, was to define my 15 weeks at training school.

"Roberts?"

Sophie responded.

A lead weight sunk to the bottom of my stomach as the realisation dawned that it could have been me. These things should always be done alphabetically. That's fair, everyone knows where they are and it always worked at school. However, I recognised that I was not at school anymore, the rules here were different from anything I ever knew before and this was not the time to question their methods.

Standing on my tiptoes and raising my hand slightly in the air, I piped up.

"I think I missed my name."

From the second I started speaking, people parted like the red sea. My face burned as every eye in the room focused on me. There was no longer a need to stand on tiptoes.

Lowering the clipboard to his side, the instructor looked me straight in the eyes and spat a single word.

"What?"

The room was quieter than an empty chapel. He must have heard me, but I repeated it nevertheless.

"I think I missed my name."

"YOU THINK YOU HAVE MISSED YOUR NAME, WHAT?!"

I did not know if he was deaf or just had a penchant for the word 'what', but he was roaring at me and beginning to change colour. A vein was throbbing in his ever-reddening neck.

I was about to shrug my shoulders in bewilderment when, looking around, I realised the situation was escalating. My fellow recruits had inched away from me, distancing themselves from the line of fire and association with me. I felt exposed and vulnerable. I needed some inspiration and in a flash, it came.

"Sir?" Rather than addressing a man of authority, it came out more like a meek question, but it at least had the effect of returning him to a more natural colour. He continued, his tone menacing and his eyes locked on mine.

"Fullen, is it?"

"Yes, that's right."

"Yes, that's right, what?!"

I began to wonder if he was being deliberately awkward or if he was actually that stupid. Maybe it was my accent. I spoke again, but slower.

"Yes, that is right, it is Fullen."

"Yes, that is right it is Fullen SIR!"

"Oh, right."

Shit. He was going purple again.

"Sir!"

He glared at me for a few more seconds before he moved his eyes back to the clipboard and read out the rest of the names.

And that was it. Before we had even completed the register on the first day, I had blown any chance of flying under the radar.

Had it not been for my indiscretion on the first day and my inability to remain serious for a prolonged period, I might have sailed through the 15 weeks of intense training. As it was though, it was less sailing and more mud wading. I felt it was largely unjustified. I was waking up at dawn every morning to suffer a torrent of physical and mental exercises, and I was passing every component. I could not understand why the training officers seemed to have a gripe with me. When I discussed this with Sophie, she suggested that I spend less time smiling and more time looking knackered and/or interested, depending on the situation. But I wanted to remain upbeat and optimistic. To me, it was a natural instinct to seek the positive in any situation. The instructors did not see things my way. In truth, I hated training school. I hated waking up every morning, knowing I would spend the day getting shouted at. I got blasted during physical training, during lectures and on the drill ground.

I struggled with the afternoon lectures. Fresh from the welcome lull of lunch, with a full stomach and the summer sun streaming through the window, it was difficult to stay attentive. I could feel my eyes drooping slowly before being rudely awakened by a barked,

"FULLEN!"

I took cover as a pen bounced off my desk.

"Wake up!"

"What the fuck are you doing?" was the background tune of the drill ground as eager to please recruits enthusiastically executed drills we had only been shown in theory. The plentiful mistakes expected from every amateur was met with apparent disdain from the instructors. There were so many collective blunders and clangers that the jingle often hummed harmlessly away. However, if "Fullen" followed that sentence, my body prepared itself for impact. My eyes would scrunch shut for a moment and I would forcibly exhale, tightening my abdominals. It was an automatic, but ineffective reaction as the only onslaught was verbal.

It was an alien environment to me and every exchange I had with an instructor seemed to land me in hot water.

I was hobbling round the drill ground when I was pulled aside by one of my favourite instructors. At 5 foot 10 inches, he was smaller than the others, the hair above his ears had begun the transition from jet black to grey and he had a kind smile that reached his eyes. He always spoke in a friendly, cordial tone.

"How are your blisters, Fullen?"

I gave the response I assumed he was looking for, "Ok thanks, Sir."

"Are they ok or are they fucking killing?"

I thought about it. I rarely swore, but I felt compelled to mirror his language.

"They are fucking killing, Sir."

"Well, if they are fucking killing, then say they are fucking killing! Report to the instructors' office at lunch to get them bandaged."

I blamed Sophie for the blisters. She had the idea to break our work shoes in over the weekend. I wore them everywhere and started the week with very little skin on the soles of my feet. We were blissfully ignorant of the fact we would barely wear shoes at training school. The overwhelming majority of each day was spent in fire boots and, in my case, pain.

The inflexible work shoes were a far cry from the trainers I donned at my last employment. The Fire Service uniform consisted of navy trousers and pale blue shirts, a black tie, epaulettes and a cap. The trousers had a sewn-in crease running the full length of each front leg. We needed to iron in a matching fold on the back and ensure a perfect line ran down each arm of our shirts.

My experience of workwear prior to the fire service had been polo shirts and tracksuit bottoms, whereas Sophie had donned skirts and blouses. That simple fact was sufficient for us to mutually conclude that she was the better ironer.

I had always regarded Sophie as the most conversant of us. She was older, more experienced, educated and seemed altogether more clued up. When it came to the fire brigade we were equally outside our comfort zone, but it took a rollicking on parade for me to realise.

Our newly established division of labour dictated that Sophie would iron both our work trousers and shirts, while I bulled our work shoes. It was a laborious task and I spent hours circling damp cotton wool balls, smeared with polish, over the toe of each shoe to create a shine.

We arrived at training school for our fourth day, immaculately pressed and proudly parading our freshly bulled shoes.

Thankfully, there was an ex-military contingent amongst us and they immediately identified our shoes as being under par.

It took their learned hands seconds to have them gleaming.

My course mates were brilliant. From the minute we met, there had been a distinct feeling of camaraderie and equality. We were all in this journey together and we worked tirelessly to ensure we all survived. Shining shoes was unfamiliar to me and classrooms were alien to others, so skills and abilities were pooled for the cooperative effort. Thanks to our course mates, Sophie and I confidently took our place on the parade ground for the morning inspection.

An instructor weaved his way amongst us and used any excuse to bark in someone's face.

"Donaldson! It is not 5 o'clock! Next time you shave, use a razor!"

"Whickham. Burn that lose thread off."

"Burrows. Did you sleep in your car? You are covered

in dog hair."

Those infractions were punished with press ups. 20 press ups for a solitary stray hair or for a clothing imperfection.

My heart pounded and my head swam with anticipation. I held my breath and swallowed hard as my mouth dried. I could feel the moisture in my hands as they formed fists at my sides, my thumbs pointing down. The ominous clack of the instructor's heels grew louder. Then I felt his breath on the back of my neck.

"Are you going somewhere, Fullen?"

"No, Sir." I was rigid, but I clenched every muscle that bit tighter, just to make sure.

"You are not thinking of getting a tram then?"

"No, Sir."

"So why do you need tramlines?"

"I don't, Sir."

"Exactly. You have two creases in each trouser leg. Put them right for tomorrow and do 20 press ups."

My shoulders, chest and arms all ached from the accumulation of three days of incessant use, but the cold concrete floor was a relief. 20 press ups were a small price to pay for the ordeal to be over.

Sophie was mortified.

"I'm really sorry, Kate. I wish I'd messed mine up instead."

"Honestly mate, it's totally fine. It's actually worked out really well." We were changing into our training kit and had little time for conversation, but I continued as I tied my laces. "See the thing is, I was dreading getting pulled up for something, but now I have, I'm not worried about it anymore."

Sophie understood a few parades later when her hair was deemed to be below her collar.

We were learning and we got there in the end, but it took us more press ups than most. I was prepared for the physical exhaustion, in so far as I expected it, but it was the state of constant vigilance that drained me. We were bombarded with information, formulas, techniques and instructions. There were rules that I didn't know existed until I was punished for breaking them. Using the wrong staircase, wandering along the corridor in a group fewer than four and walking on the drill ground.

Questions were fired incessantly throughout the day:

"What are the dimensions of a brick?"

"Give me three characteristics of water."

"Show me a sheet bend."

It was relentless.

Six

I would be mentally and physically exhausted at the end of every day and thanks to some very bad timing, my evenings were spent moving house. Our landlord had agreed a tenancy with international students, which required us to vacate the property earlier than anticipated. We were fortunate, as within two weeks of my application, a two-bedroomed council property became available. The location was ideal and within walking distance of the quayside and Newcastle city centre. However, the low-level block of purpose-built flats was far from idyllic. I hated the concrete jungle, the stench of bleach in the lifts, the dimly lit corridors and the constant drone of traffic outside. Inside, pink wallpaper adorned each wall and the floors were covered in either a peeling blue lino or a dark green carpet so infested with grime, it crunched underfoot.

I made a decision within a minute of setting foot inside.

"I am not staying here."

"We don't have a choice."

Sophie was right.

The only thing we could do was make it more habitable and homely. While the rest of our course mates returned to the restorative sanctuary of their homes, Sophie and I spent our evenings and weekends painting, fitting carpets and moving furniture.

After the first month was over, we hit the pubs and clubs in an effort to eradicate memories and be oblivious to the weeks that lay ahead. We needed to relax, switch off, and this was our outlet. Many of our friends followed a strict route every Friday night and we merged with their timetable. The stresses of the week vanished with the first enchanting gulp of lager. The delectable refreshing taste was as welcome as its anaesthetising effect. Conversations flowed and I relaxed in a sea of familiarity and contentment. It was a blissful haven from reality and I did not want it to end, but exhaustion took over. I ended up falling asleep in a nightclub and was escorted out by an amicable bouncer. Mutual friends found Sophie inside, unaware of my abrupt exit. We had planned to stay over at our new abode, to maximise our decorating time. Neither of us wanted to make the journey alone so we left together and went home to bed.

All too soon, it was Monday morning and we reported back to the Brigade Training Centre. We started at 0700 hours and lunch was always at noon. I programmed myself to just get through 5 hours, and I celebrated every half day as a success. I had assumed there would be a parade. I didn't relish getting shouted at and doing press ups, but it would eat up some time.

The locker door burst open, ricocheting as an instructor's roar pierced my positivity.

"Recruits. Training kit. Yard. Now!"

The yard. It was a flat, innocent expanse of tarmac, but I hated it. As recruits, we associated it with getting shouted at, either during physical training or drill sessions. Nothing good ever came from setting foot on it.

It stretched out to the rear of the main training centre building, approximately the size of half a football pitch. Hot fire training facilities circled the perimeter, creating an almost constant presence of smoke. A flagpole stood at the south west corner, and a flag would majestically flutter above our heads as we endured parade. Car wrecks were stored on the far side of the yard, leaning against a fence that backed onto a main road. The structures, both permanent and interim, added to the yard's oppression, creating a crater, a well of uncertainty and apprehension of which there appeared no escape.

Changing out of my immaculate uniform and shiny shoes, I felt sick. I hurried because no-one wanted to be last, but I was dreading the session that lay ahead.

It began as usual with light jogging on the spot, followed by stretching. Some people displayed a confident air. They were light on their toes, their knees thrusting up to their chest, elbows tucked in as their hands swung towards the sky, head high and shoulders back. I looked down at the tarmac. The heavy feeling in my stomach was pulling me down. My legs were weighty and my feet relayed the sentiment to the ground, acting as a magnetic force with the earth. The effort to pull away with each step was enormous and we had not even begun. I was defeating myself.

I forced myself to change my outlook as we were herded together. I had to get through this.

Raising my head, I benefited from the cool morning summer breeze.

One step at a time.

A thick yellow line extended around the entire circumference of the yard. We were told to run slowly around it in single file line, but the front runners were keen to impress and set a pace I considered fast. The back runner then had to sprint to the front.

"Fullen. Go."

I sprinted past 23 of my course mates on the outside of the circle. There were no corners to cut and I fell in line at the front. We continued to take our turn for half an hour and the line of recruits began to stretch out. It was natural given the contrasting fitness levels, but I was exasperated as my mates were negligently increasing the length of the sprint.

"Ok, right. Run in pairs and squash up." I naively thought the instructor was helping and enjoyed a few seconds respite as we ran at a comfortable pace, until,

"Right. First two. Sprint to the back. Go!"

The front two guys peeled off and ran past us to the back.

"No, you duck eggs!" Swearing was not always necessary. "Get back to the front!"

My lungs were on fire. I was relieved it had not been me.

"Sprint round the circle! Last one back 10 press ups. Go!"

They went. And we watched. We were all panting heavily, drenched in sweat. The only sound had been trainers hitting the ground almost in unison, accompanied by heavy breathing, but now exaggerated sighs were ringing out across the group. I took heart. I was not the only one suffering. I did not win my race and set about completing my press ups. I had expected them to be a welcome break, but the exercise was significantly more difficult when I was gasping for air.

"Get a move on, Fullen! Catch them up." The line of runners did not stop, the losing contestant had to sprint to catch up, leaving them at a disadvantage for the next leg. Every time I arrived at the front, I told myself it would be the last time. I was wrong on at least 10 occasions before I stopped counting. Not knowing when the pain would end was one of the hardest aspects of the brutal session.

Eventually, an hour into the session, we were told to stop running and form groups of 5. With 24 recruits, one team would be short and there was a desperate scramble to avoid being in that squad.

"First person counts to 50, next person counts to 40, next 30, 20 and 10." Counting didn't seem so bad. "Press Ups. Go"

150 Press Ups were well outside everyone's comfort zone, but there was no rustle of discontent. Instead, brows

furrowed and metaphoric sleeves rolled up as we dug deep and got each other through it. We all struggled, but while some were physically stronger, others had a powerful psyche—a mentality to keep going whatever the cost. They each had their merits.

I was at the back for every running element and I was grateful for the encouragement of the pack, but I hated feeling like a weak link. It was disheartening and lonely. However, bodyweight exercises are a great leveller and I was no longer lagging behind. I was breathing hard and my muscles were spent, every repetition felt like a monumental effort. The guy next to me threw up and buckled to the floor with exhaustion. He wiped himself down, took a few deep breaths and went again. It was then that I recognised that the supposedly weakest member had a pivotal role to play. That man was my beacon of hope, my inspiration and the reason I knew I could get through this. If he was able to keep going then I had no excuse.

We were a team. From the strongest to the weakest, we kept each other going.

A plethora of other exercises followed as motivation, determination and fortitude had to conceal the desertion of power and ability. Our legs wobbled and our heads flopped from the effort. We were all running on empty when it finally ended.

We were given three minutes to shower and assemble in the lecture room. Uncomfortably damp, we all waited for our first lecture of the day when the Commander stormed in. He was enraged.

"Who the flaming hell do you think you are?!"

Chair legs scraped the floor as we each sat back and tensed. A split second later we sank as far into our seats as possible.

"You think you have made it. Well, you flaming well have not…you are nothing. Nothing! Do you hear me?!"

We nodded. The movement was almost imperceptible. I felt that he wanted a response, but I was also trying to be invisible.

"I have been in this brigade for 28 years. I have seen things and done things that you cannot even begin to imagine…I love the fire service and I am proud to serve in it. I would fight for it with a rifle if I had to!"

He had lost me. The continued raised voice dissipated its impact and I did not understand the content of his argument. The fire service was not a physical being and I could not comprehend a scenario that required this man, armed with a rifle, to defend it. However, he was undeniably passionate and vehemently upset. He spent the best part of 10 minutes blasting us out and pulling us all to shreds before slamming the door on his way out.

It transpired that there had been an incident at a local nightclub that had brought the brigade into disrepute. The culprit was sitting in this very room and the officers were aware who it was. The guilty party had until the end of the day to come forward. We were all warned about our future behaviour and we were told in no uncertain terms that we would all be punished for one person's indiscretion. Instead of the planned lecture, we were to report to the yard in full fire kit for a morning of 'beasting' drills. These drills were so named because they served no purpose other than to exhaust and punish those involved in them.

Fire kit is designed to allow the wearer to work in intense heat and cares little for the well-being of the wearer. It's similar to wearing ski clothing in the height of summer, but without the comfort vents and technical breathability material. Heat builds up rapidly and there's nowhere for it to go. It was mid-July and standing in fire kit for three hours would have seen us sweating profusely, but that was a scenario we could only dream of.

We spent that morning rolling out fire hose and making it up again. The hose is approximately the same size as a standard swimming pool and stored as a coil to allow it to be run out quickly in an emergency. The couplings at either end allow numerous lengths to be connected together as fires are not always conveniently located at the side of the road.

Each run out involved a squat down to the hose, a motion similar to a kettlebell swing to hoist it shoulder length and then a sprint to unravel the coil. The make-up followed immediately, squatting down to begin the wind up and then a duck walk of 20 metres to guide the hose back to its original state.

You would then be permitted a second or two to stand at full height, but only to move around the other side of the hose and do it again an infinite amount of times. There were only four instructors to 24 recruits, but every attempt to straighten yourself or have a breather would result in someone being on your back.

At first, I thought it was funny. I was competent at hose running and after four weeks of being bombarded with new information, I appreciated the familiarity. However, it quickly became anything but.

My clothes had surpassed damp and yet I was still over-heating. Between my fire kit, helmet and gloves, there was nowhere for the heat to go. Every muscle was burning from the cumulative effort and I was gasping for breath. I was, in many ways, a fish out of water.

I stood up as I completed another run and glanced around. Pain and determination was etched on every face.

"Fullen! Get a move on!"

I kept going. Increasingly people were getting shouted at. It was calculated. Two deep breaths and a back stretch in exchange for your name to be hollered across the yard was worth it.

Then people started throwing up.

"You had better not be sick on my yard!" The booming, intimidating voice was followed by the unmistakable sound of someone retching.

I kept going, hopeful that this was a good indicator that we had all had enough. I was operating on autopilot now, dragging my body through every exhausting step, my mind was elsewhere…

Why had no-one come forward? This was horrific and

someone had the power to make it stop.

I froze and the hose slipped from my hand. The resulting bark went over my head.

Two more people were screamed at for having the audacity to be sick through sheer effort.

"Roberts! Are you being sick?!"

I instinctively looked round to check on my friend.

"Fullen! Don't you dare stop!"

A sickening emptiness jammed my stomach as a terrible realisation took hold. I had been involved in an incident at a local nightclub. Maybe it was me.

My mental torment took hold as lunchtime brought a temporary respite to the physical torture.

Changing out of my sodden clothes was the first opportunity I got to speak to Sophie.

"I'm going to go and speak to them."

I didn't wait for a response, but Sophie soon caught up with me and grabbed my arm.

"Why?"

I was exhausted, mentally and physically. I was mortified that my actions had caused such repercussions and I barely managed to look my best friend in the eye.

"He was probably talking about me."

Sophie had not actually been involved in the episode on Friday night and therefore could see it from a neutral perspective. Falling asleep in a nightclub could hardly be construed as an incident and neither of us could recall mentioning the fire brigade on our night out. We discussed it for a few minutes and weighed up the pros and cons before we mutually agreed to keep quiet.

Sophie and I, along with the other 22 recruits, endured an afternoon of non-stop drills in the height of summer. Our helmets, fire tunic, leggings and boots were more like torture items than safety gear. We had no breaks. You might have expected a few glances, anguished looks or questioning faces, but there was none of that. I had no doubt that internally people were querying, cursing the individual responsible, but there were no external exchanges. The truth was, that afternoon we were not given two seconds pause, the time required to catch someone's eye.

Changing out of my fire kit to report for a final debriefing in the lecture room, I was met by a totally stressed out Sophie.

"You're going to have to say something!" As the words fell out of her mouth, I stepped back in a futile attempt to distance myself from them and their consequences. Then I tried ignorance.

"Me? Why?"

Four hours of solid drilling and the fact that no-one had come forward had caused Sophie to doubt memories of Friday night.

"Well, you were involved in an incident at a nightclub."

I was indignant. "Oh, so NOW it's an incident!"

"And maybe you told the bouncer that you were tired because you've been on a training course."

"Did I?" I felt like I was going to throw up.

"I'm just saying you might have."

"Thanks, mate." It was disingenuous.

If I was going to own up, I wished I'd done it earlier. Four weeks in and although I never got off to the best start with the instructors, I had got on well with my fellow recruits. I realised very early on that I was more bothered by their opinions than those of the instructors. The shouting would subside, but respect endured. I knew which side I was on. I was happy to take my share of the rollickings as it showed that I was not getting an easy ride and I felt firmly ensconced as one of the lads.

That was about to change. Although I hated training school, I was as determined as ever to be a firefighter. If accepting responsibility was going to keep me on the course, then I had to do it.

I hunted out the head honcho. He was the most physically intimidating officer, but I also considered him to be amongst the most approachable.

"Sir," I had learned from my first day mishap. "Can I have a word?"

"Yes, but you'll have to be quick." His reply was gruff, but as he was a tall, well-built man, his voice was probably always gruff. I swallowed hard.

Sophie, having come with me for moral support, nodded for me to go on.

"The thing is, on Friday, I…"

"Well, we."

I looked at Sophie. I could have done without the

interruption, but I was grateful for her backing. I continued.

"Yeah, on Friday, we... went to The Powerhouse."

He looked confused.

Sophie helped, "A gay bar."

In the training centre bubble, I did not perceive sexuality to be an issue. However, the giant of a man stood before me was now looking totally perplexed and actually quite awkward.

He did not speak. His bewildered expression and ensuing silence were making me extremely uncomfortable. I resumed my story.

"So, I..."

Sophie loyally interjected, "We..."

"We were at The Powerhouse, a gay bar, on Friday night. I fell asleep and the bouncer asked me to leave." I did not pause for breath. The whole thing was taking too long. I just wanted it over with.

His expression was blank as he barked, "And?"

And. There really wasn't an 'and' unless there was an 'and' that I didn't remember, but I was sure I had not been that drunk.

"And, then I left."

"And why are you telling me this..."

I knew he was going to ask why it had taken me till the end of the day to come forward.

"Well, I would have told you earlier, but I honestly didn't think I did anything wrong, Sir."

He sighed, paused and stood upright. He then spent

a good few seconds looking between Sophie and I. He appeared to be deliberating his next move. Finally, he spoke.

"It wasn't you."

And with that he was gone. Probably to update the other instructors.

Attending a gay bar means nothing, but in fire brigade terms it was the equivalent of waving a rainbow flag, singing 'I am what I am' in the Castro region of San Francisco. It was inconsequential as attitudes did not change towards us. The training centre was indiscriminate as every recruit was treated with equal disdain. However, I heard via my course mates that the instructors had been curious. Female firefighters were still something of a novelty to them, but lesbians were a complete enigma and the fact that Sophie and I lived together had fuelled their imaginations.

"Why do you think your names were at the top of the list on that first day?" one recruit explained. "They were desperate to see who you were!"

I didn't like being highlighted as different, nor the idea that my private life had been the subject of speculation. Furthermore, I was irked to discover that my initial gaffe was caused by idle curiosity surrounding my sexuality. However, a conclusion had now been reached and the chapter subsequently closed, so I was happy to leave it at that.

We never did find out who was responsible for that day of drills and coming outs. As time went on, we began to suspect it was fabricated. We were never given a chance to interrogate each other. The instructors wanted an excuse to blast us out and with 24 young people hitting pubs and clubs throughout the north east, there was a good chance that an incident may have occurred so they went with that.

Six more long weeks went by. I did the work and passed the tests. However, I still found myself at the wrong end of several tongue lashings.

"What the fuck are you doing?!" was spat in my direction as I made my first attempt at a particular knot. My second attempt was not much better and I was hauled off to be shouted at.

Expletives filled the air as my instructor's face turned purple.

"People are dying in there and you are fucking about with a basic fucking knot!"

It was a serious scenario: hose was needed inside the imaginary burning building to extinguish the pretend fire. I understood the solemn significance, but I could feel an uncontrollable urge forming in my stomach. I focused on the moment and the gravity of the situation. This was the first time I had been removed from the group for the sole purpose of getting shouted at, but I felt the compulsion rising. It was in my chest. My mind tried to take me somewhere else and I swallowed hard in an attempt to suppress my natural response, but my efforts were in vain.

I laughed.

He was now apoplectic. His face inches from mine, spit rested on my cheek as he screamed at me. I have no idea as to the content of his words, I can only testify to the venom.

I had to think of something else, something that would not make me laugh. Mundane activities came to mind, doing the dishes, ironing, polishing shoes. After a few minutes, the instructor ran out of steam and spoke to me in a normal tone.

"Do you understand why it is so important?"

I looked at him. He was a decent man, doing his job. We appeared to be talking to each other with respect so I decided to chance an explanation.

"Yes, Sir. I do understand. But…"

I paused. I did not want to push it. I checked him for a reaction and took his widening eyes as permission.

"I just don't understand, if the knot is so important, why have we not done it before?"

The instructor was defensive. "Are you saying you haven't been taught how to do that knot?"

"No, Sir. I'm saying, I was shown it once, several weeks ago, but I have never actually done that knot before."

I had pushed his patience and was ordered back on the drill ground.

Within minutes, my fellow recruits were each ordered two at a time to report to various instructors placed around the yard. I later discovered it was to attempt that same knot. Out of the course of 24, only four people did it correctly. One of whom was Sophie, who somehow managed to confuse her instructor into doing it for her.

I felt that on that occasion at least, I had been exonerated.

"Fullen, wake up!" continued to reverberate around the classroom, but what the instructors could not get their heads around or argue with, was the fact that whilst I never appeared to be concentrating on the lecture in hand, I scored the highest in every written exam. On the theory side, they could not touch me. But, when I slipped to 80% in a practical exam, I was summoned to appear in front of the Commander.

If I had scored 80% in any of my degree assignments I would have been ecstatic. 80% was an A in almost any field. Needless to say, I felt aggrieved.

I was dressed in white shirt, black tie and blue dress trousers. When we were issued this uniform on our first day, we were told it was only to be worn for promotion interviews, "official bollockings" and funerals.

I had hoped it would remain in my locker until I was ready for my ascent up the ranks, but formal audiences with the Commander required it.

The commander spoke first, his voice soft but strangely unnerving.

"What is going on, Fullen?!"

I really wanted to say,

"I have absolutely no idea what you are talking about."

But, in truth I was terrified. I had not adjusted well to the militaristic way of life, calling someone 'Sir' still felt strange and although I was now immune to getting shouted at, this was different. I was flanked by two instructors and was standing opposite an older man, who had possibly just celebrated his half century. He wore a uniform similar to my own, but he also had a black cap decorated with ribbon, several medals adorned his chest and he sported a white moustache. In short, he looked like an important man. The fact that he remained seated behind his strangely small desk served to escalate his prominence.

I had nothing to say but I felt I needed to respond, so I kept it simple.

"Sir?"

This was his cue. He went on an extremely long rant about the need to maintain standards. He was so incensed that on several occasions I was grateful that the desk was just sufficiently large enough to keep his spittle out of range.

I desperately tried to focus, but equally I did not want to be in that room. As he continued to shout at me, I got to thinking...

In this particular practical exam, I was selected, apparently at random, to be number two on a standard pitch of the 10.5metre ladder. Number one gives all the orders, numbers three and four do the placement, extending and a bit of moving around. Number two does very little, bar getting the ladder to the vertical and then bracing it. Number two effectively makes up the numbers. It was impossible to score highly on enthusiasm, work rate, commanding orders or efficiency and therefore 80% would be a fairly decent score. It would indicate I had done my job effectively without being extraordinary. Being an extraordinary number two, would actually be impossible.

I shouldn't rock the boat. I'm quiet and unassuming. I hate confrontation. On the other hand, I'm a Libra. The stars conspired to make sure I fought injustice.

I nodded my way through my reprimand and tried to look thankful when I was told that on this occasion it would go no further. Eventually he stopped speaking, placed his hands on the desk, pulled himself up and leaned towards me. He looked me square in the eyes and said,

"Do you understand?"

I knew this one. It was bread and butter to anyone who had the misfortune to get shouted at.

"Yes, Sir."

"Good. You can go."

He sat back down. I stood for a second, not knowing what was expected. I hesitated and desperately resisted the urge to speak. I told myself to leave, so I turned and made for the door. I concentrated on each step, willing my feet to keep moving and my mouth to stay shut. The door got closer, I was almost free. My hand was on the handle, I pressed down. I was internally praising my self-restraint, when I involuntarily turned and opened my mouth.

"Sir."

The two instructors had gathered around the desk and blocked my view of the man in charge. As they swung round glaring at me, the important man came into view and snapped,

"Yes?"

The three men looked aghast. I had clearly broken

several military rules about addressing senior officers. It was too late to back out now. My mouth was dry, my heart was beating through my chest, but still the words came out,

"Could I just ask what the other number two's got?"

He looked down. I knew the answer from his expression. I knew that no number two scored higher than 80%. But I got shouted out of the office, told to concentrate on my own results and two days later, I was more formally chastised with a case-note, the first stage of the disciplinary procedure, seemingly for having an attitude problem.

Case-notes are only temporary black marks and it would be eliminated from my personal record in a matter of weeks, but it was a wake-up call. I kept my head down from there on in. I learned fairly quickly it was all just a game. Nothing was personal, but you had to be able to take the pressure. As intense as it was, it was nothing compared to the world of operational firefighters. Neither the job nor the training was to be taken lightly. After 15 weeks, I had complete confidence. In myself, my fellow recruits, the equipment and all the firefighters who had gone before me.

We passed out in front of all our family and friends. My parents, siblings and future sister-in-law all made the 90-minute trip from Yorkshire. It was an afternoon to exhibit our new skills. Well-rehearsed scenarios played out as performances with an accompanying narrative boomed across the loudspeaker. We each received a certificate to mark our transition from recruit to probationary firefighter. It would be a further four years before we would be considered competent.

My family stayed for photographs, a walk around the training facility and some afternoon tea served in the canteen. It was a touching and tangible show of support and I was both grateful and elated to see them.

The day was tinged with sadness as it also signalled the end of our recruits' course and the last time we would all be together. We had shared successes and failings over an intense four months, and created memories that would last a lifetime. However, we had received our postings to various stations and watches across the county, and the shift system would dictate that at any given time some of us would be on duty.

I'd felt supported throughout my course and enjoyed sharing a common objective, but I would complete the remainder of my four-year probation alone and I didn't relish the solitary journey that lay ahead.

Each station in Tyne and Wear fire brigade had 4 watches: red, white, green and blue. The colours were used to denote shifts and call signs identified stations. The four distinct teams rotated to provide 24-hour assistance.

I was happy with my placement but it was not my first choice. I had requested my nearest station. I had no intention to stay at my flat any longer than necessary, but the fire boat was located there and the additional incidents and training involved appealed to me. I was told that base did not have adequate facilities for women so I was given my second choice, a station in the west end of Newcastle. I had visited it frequently throughout my recruitment campaign, and had found the guys welcoming and the place notoriously busy.

I was pleased to see three of my fellow recruits were also assigned to the same location, one of us on each watch. We wouldn't be working together, but we were assured of a familiar face at the turnover of each shift. Approximately a quarter of the course were detailed to the red watch and some would be at stations close to mine, so our paths would undoubtedly cross at incidents.

Sophie landed her first choice and was allocated the white watch at a station in a largely well-to-do area. We would get a solid 48 hours off together and a couple of evenings every 8 days. However, I would not see the majority of my course mates for some considerable time. That night we hit south shields for a curry none of us would remember—we began drinking before we boarded the bus from training school and continued long into the night. I had survived a course that had catapulted me from my comfort zone into an extraordinary environment. That night we celebrated the end of our time at training school and the start of a new adventure as we graduated to the real world of firefighting.

Seven

The atmosphere of the fire station was a complete contrast to the training school. It was functional and unapologetic. Endeavour and industry percolated from its foundations through to the training tower that rose majestically from the station yard.

The training school demanded respect, but the fire station earned it.

Every part of the station served and proudly displayed a purpose. The offices were alive with files and paperwork. The appliance room had three bays, occupied by two gleaming red fire engines standing dutifully alongside an ambulance. Each room had a name that stated its function and there was no amalgamation of roles; the locker room, the drying room, the kit cleaning room, the dormitory, the kitchen, the lecture room, the office and the gym. There was no pomp or ceremony, everything was laid out with minimal fuss. I was the first female firefighter to be stationed there. To accommodate my arrival, a female sign had been added to the disabled toilet.

The station was practical, but brimming with character. The walls seemed to absorb laughter and it vibrated around the station. There was the familiar smell of smoke and sweat, mixed with grease and polish, but also something else. Memories suspended in the air and lay draped over the fire kit laid out in the muster bay. Jobs where lives were saved, friendships forged and tragedy avoided, resided alongside darker recollections of lives lost. There was no hint of morbid or macabre thoughts, but a distinct sign of respect and a reassurance that they would never be forgotten.

On Friday 3rd November 2000, I reported for duty at my assigned station, covering the west end of Newcastle. I was to be the latest member of Bravo Red Watch. At exactly 09:00 hours a succession of drawn out bleeps resonated around the building.

The unexpected sound caused my shoulders to draw back and my abdominal muscles engaged. My spontaneous perfect posture exposed a nervousness I was striving to keep hidden.

"That's the admin tone. It's signalling the change of shift."

I turned towards the explanation and found a friendly, professionally-tanned face. He had short brown hair and his brilliant white teeth were at my eye level. He had been introduced to me as 'Tyson'.

"Right. Thanks."

"It does that every time a message is sent down from control. We get weather warnings, road closures, that kind of thing."

"Ok, thanks." I grinned and nodded enthusiastically. I was like an eager dog, thankful for any scrap of information.

We were standing in the muster area, where every firefighters' kit was immaculately laid out. It was enveloped by the appliance room and I had my back to a perfectly polished fire engine that I was itching to ride.

Tyson showed me to the nearby printer and demonstrated how to silence the piercing tone.

"That will be one of your jobs."

It was a simple, menial task, but it assigned me a role and I was grateful for it.

Tyson continued.

"This printer is where everything comes down. Emergency calls and admin messages. If it's a fire call, it's the job of whoever gets here first. Acknowledge the call by pressing this button."

His hand hovered over a red button on a control panel.

"Right." I could do that.

"Then, shout out who the call is for and tear off the sheet. There's a duplicate underneath. Give one copy to the gaffer and one to the sub officer. Shout out the address and what type of incident it is. Then, open the appliance doors."

It had become exponentially more difficult and I made a mental note to make sure I was not first, at least for today.

There was a strange clip clop sound, like a partially hoofed pony. The gaffer's shoes announced his imminent arrival. He was flanked by two other men, the markings on their epaulettes signalled a rank.

We fell in line with the rest of my watch facing our superiors. Feet shoulder width apart, palms interlocked behind our backs.

The largest of the officers held a clipboard in fingers that resembled sausages. He had a huge bald head and a smile that filled his face. His shoulders were the size of a pig's head and his voice boomed,

"PARADE. PARADE-SHUN."

There was a single sound as 10 pairs of heels clicked together, our arms thrust down tight against our sides, thumbs pointing down.

"PARADE...STAND AT...EASE."

We resumed our original position.

It was a ten second ritual that appeared to serve no purpose, but to me it exuded professionalism and was a comforting extension from training school.

"Welcome aboard, Kate. I'm sure you will fit right in."

The giant of a man beamed while the two managers beside him smiled and nodded along.

The North East of England is famed for the warmth of the locals. Their accent can be harsh and the banter is relentless, but there is no under-current to Geordies. What you see is what you get. Their welcome was genuine, but I reacted as if they were my parents trying to get my attention at a school play.

Starting on the watch was daunting. I felt like an intruder to this tight knit group of people who all shared a bond that came from their joint experiences of extremely intense situations. Any one of them would risk their life to save another. I had my meeting with the gaffer the week before and had got off to a decent start with my initial four seconds, but on my first parade I was terrified and desperately wanted to make a good impression.

I was not sure if speaking was permitted on parade and yet I did not want to appear rude by not answering. The moment passed as I deliberated and he proceeded to designate jobs.

I was nominated to ride as the entry control officer. I was to ride in the middle of the first fire engine sandwiched between my colossal junior officer, known as 'Cat', and Tyson. Back in 2000, the entry control officer was deemed an essential role to monitor the safety of the breathing apparatus (BA) wearers. However, my appointment to that role was primarily so the gaffer could keep an eye on me. It was common practice and most of my fellow recruits would have taken up an identical riding position at least for their first few weeks. I was fresh out of training school and extremely enthusiastic. I would have preferred to be a wearer, but I had an actual riding position and a purpose on a fire engine. I was desperate for my first call.

It came at 09:03hrs. Three minutes into my operational firefighter career, I was heading to a confirmed Persons' reported: that meant the caller had categorically stated that people were trapped inside.

No amount of training can fully prepare you for the real

thing. Getting shouted at in training school was irksome. The smoke and the heat made it physically stressful, but even when you were getting lost in wardrobes, you knew you could laugh about it afterwards and no one would get hurt. This was different. My actions would have consequences. If I failed to do my job properly people could get hurt, or worse.

I had no time to do anything en-route aside from putting on my fire kit. The BA wearers either side of me had managed to put on their fire kit, fit cylinders of compressed air to their backs, grab various bits of equipment, as well as direct me.

"Don't worry," Tyson said. His voice was firm, but reassuring. "Just help with the hose reel, and then stand by the gaffer. That way, if he needs you, he knows where you are."

It sounded simple enough. As much as I found it weird calling anyone 'Gaffer' it was easy to remember and I knew who he was, unlike most of my workmates. I tried to look confident.

Getting ready in the back of a fire appliance was harder than I thought, especially with three of us competing for arm space. The driver expertly navigated the busy streets and we did not slow once. Whilst the others braced themselves for the corners, I spent large parts of the journey being swung from one BA wearer to the other.

Sooner than expected, we arrived at the Old Peoples' Home. The wearers jumped off and I headed for the back locker, which housed the hose reel. The crew from our second appliance joined me and the three of us pulled the hose reel through the doors and along the corridor, until we were stopped by the smoke. The BA wearers took it from there, protected by their masks and compressed air. The gaffer, protected only by his moustache, followed them. I watched as the three of them disappeared into the smoke. Then in a flash of panic, I remembered the words "stay by the gaffer," but I had neither a moustache nor a death wish, so was reluctant to follow them.

The guys who had helped me with the hose reel had gone. I was the entry control officer and was responsible for the safety of the two wearers. So, I reasoned, I would go back and set up the entry control board.

My instructors at training school had left us with no doubt as to the importance of the board.

"This board might save your life!"

It was an exaggeration. As an inanimate object, it lacked the necessary credentials for heroism. However, it was designed to store critical information.

In addition to the compressed air, a breathing appa-ratus wearer carries several pieces of ancillary equipment including a personal distress unit. The unit was armed by the removal of a tally and would send out an audible dis-tress signal should the wearer activate the button or remain motionless for a period of 30 seconds.

The tally contained the wearers name and the volume of air present in their cylinder. The entry control board is used to store these tallies and monitor the location of each team. It is also used to determine how long the wearer has before their air runs out. A ten-minute safety margin was mandatory and all wearers had to return before their low-pressure warning whistle sounded. Failure to do so would constitute an emergency situation and an immediate redeployment of all teams to that wearer's location.

Once outside, everything seemed surreal. Everyone had a job and was busy doing it. There was no hint of panic, except from me; my heart was pounding in my chest. The BA board was stowed in the front locker, between two BA sets, and held in place by a single strap. Done calmly it can be removed in a few seconds. I wrestled with it until I felt a tap on my shoulder.

"You ok, Kate?"

I stopped wrestling and turned to face Tyson. Behind him, one of the guys was administering oxygen to an elderly gentleman. The job was over and I, with my head in a locker, had missed it. The whole thing was over in only a few minutes. There was nothing left for me to do except make up the hose reel. On the more relaxed return journey I learned three important lessons:

Firstly, the BA board that we used routinely at training school was seldom deployed in the real world. We were not always afforded the time and often, the job was over before the board could be set up.

Secondly, the hose-reel was my main priority. I did not feel I contributed to saving that man's life, but the lads explained that each of us has a job. Regardless of how insignificant you think that job is, every component is essential and contributes to the overall result. I felt better.

And finally: never take your fire kit off before you get back to the station. Before I knew it we were summoned on the radio and were off again.

Eight

I did not have to wait long before I got my first BA experience. Mid-afternoon on my first dayshift we attended a derelict house fire. On arrival, we found black smoke pouring out from a two-storey building. The heat reached me as I climbed down from the fire engine. It was a comfortable warmth, as the front yard provided a ten-metre safety margin.

Flames danced from the eaves, while a monstrous ball of orange swelled from the ground floor. I watched as the fire appeared to rhythmically constrict and expand, as if it were a mouth feeding on the dark toxic gasses. Ominous crackling spat from the ravaged home as furniture was devoured. Fire has an insatiable appetite.

As there was no immediate life risk, this was considered a good opportunity to give me some guided experience. So, after I ran out the hose-reel, the gaffer instructed me to put on a breathing apparatus set. This was it; I was going in.

I could not put the set on fast enough, literally. In my elevated state, I struggled with the straps and the mask. I debated the order of what went on first to increase my speed and got everything tangled up. However, in seconds, I calmed myself down and got ready. The other two wearers were waiting just inside. At training school, every entry was made through a door, but the only access to this particular property was through a small window on the ground floor. I did not foresee any problems until I put my hands on the ledge. Then I realised I was in trouble. I was not scared for my life, but I was terrified of losing my dignity in front of my colleagues. The extra weight of the cylinder would try and pull me backwards, there was nothing to step on and even if I did haul myself up, the cylinder would get stuck on the top of the window. I had always considered those cylinders of compressed air lifesavers, but at that very moment, I wanted nothing more than to throw it off and dive head first into the flames. At least inside the smoke would provide adequate cover from the watching eyes outside. Somebody asked if I wanted a hand up, but I declined. This was my first opportunity to prove myself and I didn't want them to think they had to help me along. If I wanted to be treated as an equal, I would have to act as one. Whatever happened, however much of an idiot I looked, I wanted to show them I could stand on my own two feet.

The window was higher than it was wide. To give myself the best chance of fitting through, I would have to go through on my front. Any delay could be construed as cowardly. So, with a deep breath of my compressed air, I hauled myself up and threw myself head first through the window.

The cylinder slid through with me; it had taken up less room than I had accounted for and I clattered into a heap on the floor at the feet of my two fellow BA wearers. I was suddenly extremely grateful for all those hours of physical training. If I had got wedged in that window, I would have never lived it down. As it was, I was in and putting aside all thoughts of how I would get out. I concentrated on the job in hand.

This was uncharted territory. I had worked in smoke and heat before, but it had been controlled. Here the flames were all over. It was red hot and I could not see my hand, let alone my BA team. We worked our way along the wall until we located and extinguished the fire. There were several seats of fire on the ground floor and we had to be sure they were all properly extinguished before we could advance to the first floor.

The staircase had partially burned away so each step had to be carefully checked before we could proceed. Similarly, the upstairs floorboards had been severely weakened. We needed to open the windows to effectively ventilate and clear the fire gases, but the floor would not stand the weight of the three of us. As the lightest, it made sense for me to go. I kept close to the wall where the boards were stronger. The room was still thick with smoke, but I knew that if I kept my left hand on the wall, I would eventually come to a window. Checking each step as I went, I inched along the wall. One wrong step and I would be through the floorboards. My safety was not my primary concern. My watch had welcomed me with open arms and treated me as one of their own. However, they had never worked with a woman before. In my mind, there were bound to be doubts as to whether or not I was capable and I was desperate to prove I was.

I felt my hand touch glass. I had made it. I fumbled with the lock and prised it open. The unmistakable whir of an industrial fan started up outside and I could imagine it being wheeled to the front door. The use of the positive pressure ventilation fan was still in its infancy, but the benefits were evident. In seconds, the smoke cleared. I could see my mates and the gaps in the floorboards. The process had to be repeated in the other rooms, but we shared the responsibility, each taking separate rooms, until the property was completely clear of smoke. I had passed my first test. It was fantastic, feeling like part of the watch. For the next few minutes I was jubilant, but then I was faced with the task of getting back through the window.

We could have made a bigger opening, even knocked a door down. The problem was, by doing that we would be inviting more potential arsonists to have a go. If we can use the same entrance they did, it makes things easier for the boarding-up team.

I busied myself with the hose-reel and bought enough time for one of the other wearers to go first. He was helped up and crew members assisted him from the other side. I learned another valuable lesson: accept help.

It made sense. We had people spare who could assist. They were not offering to help because of my gender. It was just deemed more practical to help rather than watch someone dive head first and land in broken glass. Lesson learned.

The day started winding down at 16:00 hours. We washed the fire engines, mopped the floors and emptied the bins throughout the station. I had been bombarded with information throughout the shift and I welcomed the cathartic routine of the final hour. With 20 minutes to go however, I felt lost. There were no jobs left to do and everyone had sloped off somewhere. I paced the station and bumped into members of the oncoming white watch.

"You must be Kate…How was it?… Are the lads treating you ok?… We call them Baywatch you know. There are some handsome guys on your watch!"

I laughed and felt a flood of warmth. The kindness and affability that had emanated from my watch was now being extended from other watches on the station. The whole atmosphere was incredible; there was nowhere else I would rather be.

As I cycled home, visions of the day's events flashed through my mind. I could not wait to relay every detail to Sophie, but frustratingly she was starting her first night shift. It would be another 40 hours until I saw her and even then, coming off two nightshifts, she may be more preoccupied with sleep.

It was 17:30 on a Friday night. All of my friends would be out, so I rang my parents. They had a habit of asking the same questions, but for the first time I was grateful that I got to have the same conversation twice.

High on adrenaline, unable to focus on the TV, I paced around the flat rerunning the day's events in my mind until the effects eventually wore off.

Nine

"Nice bike, but you look like a bag of hammers." James' version of 'good morning' relaxed me immediately as I cycled into the yard for my second day.

James was my senior hand. The title was given to the firefighter with the most time in the job and had nothing to do with age, but James was in his late thirties and happened to be the eldest. We were a young watch, but there was no lack of experience. Three guys had been riding fire engines for over fifteen years. Furthermore, they had served their time at the busiest station in the country.

James was my height, but his personality filled any room. He was well liked and respected by his peers and the Gaffer. He was a joker and an excellent practical firefighter. I would learn a lot from him.

I enjoyed the feeling of familiarity as we stood on parade. It provided a sense that I had been here before and I was gradually acclimatising to my new surroundings. However, it was Saturday and the weekend brought an additional list of jobs that formed the weekly work routine.

The appliance room floor was cleaned, the contents of every cylinder checked, spare batteries were charged and every conceivable piece of equipment inside the station was tested, from the tyre pressure gauge through to the ring cutter. The emergency lighting, fire alarm call points and gym equipment were all scrutinised. It took up most of the morning, but I felt I knew the station inside out by the time we had finished.

We had just sat down to lunch when we were called to a fish and chip shop fire.

The incident was visible as soon as we left the station. Plumes of black smoke billowed across the road. It was so thick it made driving on the main road virtually impossible. I had become accustomed to working in smoke and darkness, relying on other senses to navigate my way, but James, our driver, did not have that luxury.

We were soon engulfed by toxic fumes. From my seat in the rear cab it appeared that we were piloting blind and I assumed we would have to stop and make the rest of the journey on foot.

The building was in a densely-populated area, a high street littered with fast food for every culture. James recognised that we needed the water and equipment on hand so he took advantage of fleeting wind driven clearings and inched us through. Our flashing blue lights were practically redundant and the blanket of fire gases had caused cars to stop in their tracks, but James negotiated both the conditions and other road users to ensure we arrived directly outside the shop. It was a corner unit with a pedestrianised street to its left and a wide pavement around the front. Intensely black, voluminous smoke cloaked the footpath and flames danced in the darkness. A handful of individuals were rooted, watching the drama unfold, but for the majority of the community it was business as usual.

The tunnel of smoke did not deter people walking through, nor did the flames or the intense heat cause them to cross the road. Hanging baskets were being tended to only several feet from the shop door.

Our arrival caused a greater stir than the fire itself. People stopped using the path immediately in front of the shop and we were afforded a clear walkway. There were flats above the shop that needed searching and there were concerns about the potential of the fire spreading to neighbouring properties.

Adam directed as if he was the conductor of an orchestra. A brief exchange with the shop's owner told him everything he needed to know.

"The fryers are at the back!" Cat and Tyson nodded an acknowledgement and then disappeared into the building.

"You two," he grabbed the lads from the second appliance, "put a set on. You're going in."

It was the words every firefighter wanted to hear. The two guys vamoosed and grabbed their breathing apparatus sets as if they were worried that Adam would change his mind.

I was on my gaffer's shoulder, desperate to be deployed,

but he had other ideas.

"Kate, set up the Entry Control Board."

It was not the role I wanted, but I remembered the advice from the earlier incident. The board was only used at larger incidents, where more control was needed and the numbers of wearers increased. In my mind, this was the definition of a big job.

My heart raced as I grabbed the board. My hands shook inside my gloves and my stomach, chest and throat felt strangely empty as self-doubt surfaced.

I had spent my entire life playing at things. I played all manner of sports, but had quit when they became too serious. I frittered 3 years at university playing at being a student. I even expended large amounts of time playing at being different versions of myself.

What if I had just been playing at being a firefighter? What if I liked the idea but could not actually see it through when it became serious? This was real life and I had to engage with it.

I assembled the control board on its tripod and was clutching 4 tallies from the wearers' personal distress units. They were each correctly labelled with their surnames and cylinder contents. It was my second day and I was just about getting to grips with first names and nicknames. Positioning the wearers into their correct teams was a feat in itself.

I then had to calculate the working duration of the cylinders for each of the four firefighters who had entered the job. I was confident in my ability to carry out basic calculations, but the consequences of error were far greater than a red cross or a 'see me' and I triple checked every answer.

Within minutes, I had completed all the necessary information and was monitoring the progress of the crews through regular radio contact. I was successfully utilising the skills that I had learned at training school for a bona fide incident and it felt electrifying. It was the first time I had been left entirely on my own and I had proved, to myself at least, that I could do this.

At that moment, a third fire engine arrived carrying four people I had never met before.

Two firefighters jumped down from the back cab.

One pulled the hose reel to the side door as the other made his way to me.

"Alright." It was a greeting, rather than a question. "You must be Kate. I'm Gaz."

"Hey Gaz."

"These are ours." He handed me two tallies. "I think we're going upstairs, we're just waiting for our gaffer to speak to yours."

I looked across and saw Adam talking to a much taller gentleman. The exchange was brief and the towering figure strode back towards us. He nodded an acknowledgement to me and addressed his crew.

"Ok guys, we're going upstairs. Search the flats. Left hand search."

Touch is our primary sense in a fire situation and the walls are our only point of reference to where we are. Search patterns involve one member of the crew keeping a hand on a wall. If they kept their left hand on the wall on the way in, they could turn around, place their right hand on the wall, and it would lead them out. If we had plans of the building or an idea as to where a casualty was, we could pick the most efficient search pattern. In cases such as this, where we had neither, it was a 50/50 choice.

I took the tallies from Gaz, inserted them into the board, and wrote 'Upstairs. Left Hand Search'. We tested the radios and I assisted them with the hose reel up the steps. Then they were gone.

Gaz updated me across the radio periodically. They were making good progress and had searched several rooms.

"Bravo one," my radio crackled. It was Gaz.

"Bravo one, go ahead."

I waited for a response.

Silence.

I tried again.

"Bravo one to Firefighter Metcalfe, go ahead."

Still nothing.

I tried again and again with the same response.

I visualised my instructor from training school barking a question:

"What constitutes a BA emergency?"

The list was indelibly marked in our heads.

"An activation of a personal distress unit... if someone failed to return before their low-pressure warning whistle activated...if a wearer appeared in distress...a sudden breakdown in communications…"

The shit had hit the fan.

In line with our procedures, I would have to declare a BA emergency. Control would send additional fire engines and all available teams would be redeployed to assist their stricken brother.

My mind was swimming. I scanned the scene, looking for an anchor.

Flames were still licking out of the shop, thick black smoke billowed across the road. The drivers were desperately locating hydrants to ensure a constant supply of water. Police had arrived to direct the traffic and I noticed an ambulance on standby. In the midst of this disaster scene, a BA wearer emerged covered in white powder. The dry powder extinguisher had apparently exploded in the heat. Unlike yesterday, there was not a single person on hand to help.

I was only halfway through my second shift as a firefighter and I had an impossible call to make. The safety and welfare of the wearers was my main concern. I would stick to the procedure and be accountable for any consequences.

"What is the latest?"

I turned to face the formidable officer in charge of the third appliance, wanting information on his crew.

I explained we had lost communications and took a step away from him. My burden was now his and I did not want it back.

Craning my neck, I watched as he puffed his cheeks.

"Where were they?" Raising his eyebrows and widening his eyes, he looked down at me in a way that could have been construed as condescending. However, I gratefully took it to mean 'I will sort out this mess'.

I knew the answer, but I used the control board as an excuse to break eye contact.

"They were upstairs, on a left-hand search and they had searched three rooms."

"Right. One minute."

He went upstairs and briefly disappeared from sight before calling down

"They're fine."

I exhaled in relief and felt my shoulders relax as my senior provided a passing explanation.

"It's the radios. They're fucking crap."

Communications became a recurring problem. With alarming regularity, the radios would fail while you were inside a job, completely cut off. Withdrawing to pass messages was not always practical. It was often a case of just making do. The communications issue was far from ideal, but the old hands could recall times before radios were used. Confidence in yourself and your crew far outweighed the need for confidence in your radio.

The incident was effectively wrapped up within another ten minutes. The fire was extinguished, the smoke was cleared and the upstairs flats were all declared empty. I surveyed the calm, efficient and methodical closure and imagined the contradictory carnage if I had actually made the BA Emergency call.

I returned the tallies to the wearers as they withdrew from the job and returned the control board to its designated locker. My adrenaline levels had subsided and I was aware of my empty stomach. As I climbed into the cab, I pictured my half-eaten soup and sandwiches and was pleased we were only minutes away from a reunion.

"Where are you going?"

I turned and saw Tyson. His soot smeared face made his teeth whiter and he shot me a friendly smile.

I just sat there and smiled at him, expecting a joke to follow.

Cat appeared behind him, his booming voice alerting everyone in earshot.

"You don't think we're finished do you? The real work starts now!"

I looked out the cab window and saw firefighters armed with axes, shovels and ceiling hooks marching into the steaming, charred remains of a shop. Most of those guys had been grafting hard while I was kitted out in a tabard, filling in a board.

Shit.

This did not look good.

I laughed to buy some time.

"No. Course not. I was just…" I scanned the cab, my hands fumbled around. I was floundering. I needed something quick.

"I was just getting a…" I blindly patted the seat behind

me and with enormous relief I stumbled on the perfect item to fit my cover story, "…torch!" I stepped down, carrying my trophy, and joined the others inside.

The chip shop had transformed from a viable business to a smouldering, burned out shell. It was uncomfortably hot and I could feel the moisture building on my skin. I could taste the smoke as it burned my throat. Clouds of steam poured from the walls and small wisps of smoke seeped out from joints and crisp wooden frames.

"Right lads. Let's get to work." It was Cat. "Oh and Kate, sorry!"

I was not offended by generic terms, and in a way they helped me feel included. I didn't want to be the odd one out, but I smiled warmly at him. He was acknowledging me and I appreciated that.

I was also grateful for the minuscule delay in getting to work as I had absolutely no idea what we were going to do. At training school, we dealt with the fire. The aftermath had not even occurred to me. Thankfully, Cat appeared to read my mind.

"The whole thing has to come down. The ceiling, the door frames and the stud walls." I nodded, despite never hearing the word 'stud wall' before. "We need to make sure the fire hasn't got in behind."

"Ok." I grabbed a large axe that had been propped against the wall.

It suddenly occurred to me that I had never handled an axe before. I feigned confidence and made for the nearest door frame. My first swing bounced back at me, throwing me slightly off balance.

I paused and focused on looking straight ahead. I sensed everyone else was preoccupied with their tasks. Thankfully no-one seemed to notice.

Taking a wider grip for my second attempt, I carefully aimed the axe head into the edge of the timber surround. It landed on its target and became stuck.

"What the… " James paused, his eyes twinkled, "…are you doing?"

He was amused and I took heart in his smile. His eyes had widened as if they had feasted on an undiscovered wonder as he continued,

"It's not a toffee apple, you know!"

I laughed, but his outburst had drawn attention and I met my Gaffer's steely blue eyes. My cheeks burned. I was not covering myself in glory.

"Have you ever used an axe before?" James asked kindly, as he wrangled it from the door.

"No," I shook my head resignedly. I wished I had, but equally I could not imagine a scenario when I would have had a reason to.

"Don't worry about it."

I was grateful for James' words and the fact that everyone else had returned to their demolition duties.

He demonstrated the correct use of the axe and patiently watched as I tried again.

"That's it!" He patted me on the shoulder as he resumed

his task. "You'll get there."

I felt as if I was under scrutiny, both as a new recruit and as a female and I was gutted that my technique with the axe had been highlighted. Desperate to show myself in a more positive light, I threw myself into the clear up operation.

I homed in on jobs that required more graft than skill: shovelling up debris, pulling smouldering remains outside and tugging the plaster from the ceiling. These forced me into the thick of it and by the time I emerged from the shop, every inch of me was covered in black soot.

On our return to the station, I jumped off to open the doors.

Tyson joined me, laughing at my appearance.

"The Gaffer said you look like something out of the black and white minstrels."

I had no idea what or who the minstrels were so I kept quiet, but I felt uneasy. In many ways I had led a sheltered life, surrounded by people who shared my beliefs and ideals. Fairness, equality and mutual respect have always been important to me. As a young teenager, angered by the BBC's description of a man, I voiced my feelings in our front room.

"They shouldn't say a black man. They never say a white man, they just say man. It's like they're saying that white is normal and black is different." I was incensed, but my family simply raised their eyebrows slightly and nodded for a nanosecond worth of reflection. I seethed as I realised it would join the list of things I did not like, but was incapable of doing anything about.

In 2000, things should have been different. The Race Relations (Amendment) Act had come into force, public bodies now had a general duty to promote race equality and yet casual racism was clearly accepted in my new place of work. It made me uncomfortable. Aside from going against my beliefs, marginalising others because of differences did not bode well for me, but I lacked the strength to challenge it. Above all else, I wanted to fit in.

Tyson continued,

"He said it was good to see you getting involved. Well done."

My relationship with the Gaffer was complicated. I respected him as a boss and was desperate to gain his approval, but I didn't like the way I felt in his presence. . He was aloof, judgemental and quick to find fault. I lost my spirit around him. My energy, enthusiasm and love of the job was replaced with a fear of failure and a consuming need to exceed his expectations.

Adam had an incredible air about him. He was slightly taller than me with white hair and an average build. It was not his physical appearance that set him aside. His decision to only speak when it was necessary granted him an attentive audience whenever he chose to articulate exactly what was on his mind. He had the unyielding respect of the dozen men on his watch, and his reputation stretched brigade wide. The second-hand scant compliment from a man I respected and feared in equal measure was a huge deal for me.

I was euphoric as we changed our fire kits and cleaned

our boots.

"The next call could be to an elderly person with a pristine carpet," was the reason the instructors had given at training school.

Cylinders were charged and all the equipment cleaned. Finally, the sandwiches were wrapped up to take home.

Ten

The fire brigade shift system was two days, then two nights, these combined were commonly referred to as a set. Each set was followed by four days off, although finishing at 09:00 hours meant you actually worked nine hours on your first day 'off'. The shift system is great and it does allow for plenty of time off, but we still work 48 hours in an eight day period, which equates to a 42 hour week. I started on my watch on 3rd November, which meant my first nightshift was the 5th November, Bonfire night.

The Green Watch were working the dayshift, which was due to finish at 17:00 hours. However, it was over an hour into our shift before they were relieved. The fire calls were incessant and the duty watch needed a lull before they could return the fire appliances to the station and hand over.

While we waited for The Green Watch to return, we ensured all the BA cylinders were charged and other routine jobs were completed. We cleared the half-eaten lunch plates and a few of the lads started preparing some food for later. Chilli, bolognese, lasagne and curries are the basic dishes of most fire station messes—meals that can be created quickly and reheated several times.

Despite the fact that we did not stop all night, the jobs themselves were of little note. Car fires, wheelie bin fires, general 'rubbish' fires and many false alarms to bonfires. However, it was my first experience of anti-social behaviour aimed at firefighters. The Gaffer used all his experience and did his best to keep the locals happy. He would not deliberately incite bad feeling and used common sense to determine which fires to put out and which to leave. If it looked safe and if there was a responsible adult present, he would leave it. Unfortunately, there were occasions, like when someone added a pressurised cylinder to the bonfire, that we had to put them out. Several times that night we were attacked. Bricks, fireworks, bottles and various other missiles were thrown, sometimes by kids as young as six.

Prior to that night, I hadn't realised that there were sections of society that were so against emergency services. The very nature of policing will inevitably draw bad feelings, but I couldn't understand why the fire and ambulance service got such a raw deal. We weren't there to judge, we attended simply to help and we treated every single person with the same degree of care.

During that night, we attended a car fire at the end of a cul-de-sac. Missiles were thrown as we extinguished the fire, and I for one was pleased when we made our exit. However, our only way out was blocked by a few dozen youths. The police were called, but the appliance suffered considerable damage. On the busiest night of the year, a front-line appliance was out of action for over an hour as all the equipment had to be taken off and moved to a spare appliance. These spare appliances tended to be slower and less efficient. There were also storage problems, so decisions had to be taken as to what gear we would have to do without. One mindless set of youths had put others in jeopardy. Their neighbours, friends and relatives now had reduced fire cover at a time when they needed it most. Fortunately, that night we got away with it.

I survived my first bonfire night and had eight hours to eat and rest before I was due back at work.

The second night of my first set was equally as busy, but this time I spent most of the night pumping water out of people's homes. A local village had flooded and we were sent as part of a makeup. Makeup, in fire brigade terms, is when the officer in charge of the incident deems it necessary to request more appliances and additional resources. Even with my limited experience, it told me two things before I got there: It was definitely a job and a fairly big one at that.

There were already several appliances in attendance when we pulled up, and by the looks of things they had been there a while. A Divisional Officer was in charge and was directing proceedings. The atmosphere here was calmer than any of the other jobs I had been to. The water was already in the houses. The damage had been done. Now it was a clean-up operation and it was going to be protracted. People were pacing themselves for a long night.

The first thing I noticed was the hose, it was all over the place. To this day, I have never seen so much hose laid out. Throughout the village, hose was run out from the houses to the river. Adam Thornton stepped off the appliance, took a look around and ordered all the hose to be made up. This was the first time I was aware of how much standing he had in the brigade. His senior officer never questioned him and all the hose was made up. At first, I thought he was mad. The residents looked bewildered, as we appeared to be packing up while their property was still a foot underwater, but the gaffer had seen the source of the problem. A flooded field was draining into the neighbouring properties. Hose was run out from the field to the river and we successfully stopped any more water reaching the houses. Several hours later, the field was empty and the clean-up operation could begin. Each house was drained and as the sun began to rise on another day, we packed up and returned to the station. We were there for almost six hours. Reliefs are normally sent after three hours, but in cases such as severe flooding, the brigade can be so stretched that there are simply no appliances spare. We got back just in time to wash the appliances down and have some breakfast.

I will always remember my first set. I was exhausted when I left at 09:00 hours, exactly 96 hours after I stood in my first operational parade. I was desperate for some sleep, but equally I could not wait for another 96 hours to pass. I was hooked and desperately wanted to be back at work to see what my next set had in store.

Eleven

On 11th February 2000, targets for the recruitment, retention and career progression of women in the Fire Service in England and Wales were announced. By that point, women made up 1% of the total number of operational firefighters, a little over 500 women, compared to 48,000 men. The new guidelines stated that by April 2002, 4% of operational firefighters should be women, rising to 9% in 2004 and 15% by April 2009.

Quoted in The Guardian the following day, Home Office minister Mike O'Brien said, "There is no reasonable justification for such low numbers of female firefighters. These challenging, but achievable targets will ensure that equality is given the importance it deserves within every brigade. Protecting the public is paramount. There can be no question that standards will be lowered just to increase the number of female firefighters. Firefighting has high physical demands and brigades have a responsibility to ensure that the best candidates are selected.

"While some sneer about 'political correctness', this is

really about a modern fire service that seeks the best fire-fighters and does not discourage them because they are women."

As I joined the fire service four months after the publication of those targets, I cannot be certain that my selection was not influenced by them. However, I spent my formative years in the fire service, blissfully unaware of their existence. Female firefighters did not flood recruitment. There may have been a steady stream of one or two a year, but they slipped quietly onto watches and were absorbed by the workforce.

James spoke for the majority of firefighters when he expounded his interpretation of equal opportunities: "I don't care if you are black or white, male or female. All I care about is, if the shit hits the fan, will you get me out?" He nodded at me. "I believe you will."

The facts were, the Fire Service was dominated by white, heterosexual men. The chance of me working alongside a female firefighter was negligible as there were six of us spread across a workforce of 1000 and I was the only one attached to the red watch. Equally demoralising, the contingent of Black and Minority Ethnic (BME) was equally sparse. Figures published by the Audit Commission in January 2006 stated that only 2.1 per cent of all Fire and Rescue authority staff were from BME communities. On top of this, there were only two openly gay firefighters in our brigade—0.2% of the workforce.

Despite these demoralising statistics and the greater

systemic issues they represented, I appreciated how welcome the lads made me feel from the outset and their uncomplicated take on my appointment. Fitting in was easy. I worked hard, listened and kept my head down. I was judged entirely by my own actions and welcomed accordingly. Adam kept his promise and never made me another cup of tea.

Mornings were spent in the station yard. The Gaffer was adamant that we did not do drills simply to be good at drills. They were there to replicate real life situations and he designed them so they would challenge us and make us better equipped to deal with any eventuality.

At training school we practiced standard ladder and hose drills, taken directly from a drill book. Each crew member was assigned a number which corresponded to a specific role within the drill. Number one would give the orders, number two was the driver, numbers three, four and five did the leg work. The higher the number, the greater the workload. As recruits we would surreptitiously count along the line, trying to gauge our number and mentally rehearse our role. It was all new to us and the drills were a way to instil rudimentary techniques. However, the training centre environment was purpose built. Every ladder pitched to the second or third floor of the drill tower was set on perfectly flat ground, with no washing lines or overhead cables in sight.

In the real world on the other hand, there's no such thing as 'standard'. Whether it was the access, the weather, the surrounding risks, or unforeseen circumstances, no two jobs were the same. To think otherwise could have dangerous consequences.

Given that I had started on station around bonfire night, I quickly became accustomed to what we termed 'rubbish fires'—this wasn't a critique as to the standard of fires, but rather a description of what the fires contained. I had attended at least a dozen such incidents in my first two sets, which all went without trouble. So, when we got called out to one in the middle of a field, I admit to being complacent. I set about kicking the debris, pulling it apart, while my mate sprayed it with water. Suddenly, I felt my foot go from under me, someone grabbed my arm and I was flung backwards. I lay stunned on the sodden grass and watched the rubbish disappear from sight. It had been laid out over an open manhole. We had been set up.

I had witnessed the events of bonfire night and experienced assaults on our crew. It was generally opportunists and kids acting up in front of their mates. However, this was a pre-planned cowardly and sinister plot to injure. In the years since, I have attended house fires where razor blades have been stuck on handrails, floorboards have been cut away and holes have been covered by rugs. Moving in smoke, heat and darkness we rely heavily on our sense of touch to negotiate hazards. Our safety procedures were cruelly being used against us.

There was nothing standard about our job and there was nothing standard about Adam's drills. They were designed to make you think. It was always a worst-case scenario, a catastrophe that would be accentuated by a lack of equipment and injured personnel. Thankfully, in 17 years, I have never been to a job that has come close to what the gaffer managed to dream up.

On one occasion, Adam had asked for just the one fire engine to be taken around the back for the drill session. The second pump remained in the appliance bay. After an hour and a half of various situations and exercises, the gaffer detailed the final 'job'. It was, as always, a scene worthy of a disaster movie.

"The 10.03 direct train from Edinburgh to London has derailed." Adam patted the drill tower wall, indicating it was now a battered carriage.

There was more: "The train is packed with passengers who have crammed into this one carriage as there is a fire at either side of the train."

It made sense. The drill tower was only four metres wide and lacked the capacity to mimic an entire train.

"A petrol tanker has crashed here." Adam walked to a point in the yard about 10 metres away. "The spill will reach the train in minutes."

As if that was not bad enough, a chasm had opened up in the exact vicinity of the incident.

Imaginary chasms and craters often opened up on our drill ground, along with shark infested custard. It meant using a ladder as a makeshift bridge and carrying all the equipment along it.

With one fire engine still parked in the appliance bay,

we struggled with limited equipment and water. However, we recognised that further resources were not always available so we improvised. Eventually the spill was declared contained, the fire extinguished and the casualties retrieved. Job complete, we filed back in line.

I did not see it coming.

The Gaffer had gone beetroot, his white moustache twitched and he was visibly shaking with rage.

"What the fuck were you thinking?! It's fucking basic!" He flung his hand in the direction of our second appliance.

"There's a fire engine parked around the corner! Fucking use it!"

Whilst I was checking for hidden fire engines, my course mates were busy practising for our upcoming probationary assessment. It consisted of standard drills which I hadn't done since leaving training school.

I figured that preparation for my exam didn't come under the banner of small talk, so I approached the gaffer and asked if it would be possible to do a run through of some standard drills prior to my test day. He agreed that practice would be beneficial, but the only time he was willing to set aside was the week before my exam. I'm not sure if it was design or coincidence, but that was my allocated period of leave. I couldn't afford to pass up the opportunity, so I came into work on my day off.

It was a warm, sunny, spring morning, perfect for a walk through of the ladder and hose drills that would be on my exam. Unfortunately, Adam had other ideas. I formed part of a three-person team. Wearing breathing apparatus, we were to haul lengths of hose, charged with water, up the 13.5 metre ladder and down the internal stairway. We would then negotiate a crawling section and locate the casualties before retracing our steps, carrying both the dummies and hose to safety. It was a ship scenario and would not figure on my exam. It served little purpose other than to exhaust those of us involved.

Infuriated and drained, I left the station frustrated that I had lacked the courage to speak up and walk away. I was also jealous, for while my fellow recruits were afforded adequate rehearsal for their impending assessments, I had landed a gaffer that had absolutely no desire to be good at drills.

Thankfully, the following week I passed my exam with 93 per cent. I'd successfully negotiated my first hurdle and was ecstatic, but I remained envious of my course mates.

They had settled so well into their new watches that many of them were 'acting up' to the role of leading fire-fighter. The additional money for acting up, while still on probationary wages, was significant. So significant in fact, I approached the subject with Adam. I entered his office and left less than two minutes later with a very clear notion that it would be some considerable time before I mentioned the words 'acting up' again.

In fairness to Adam, he had a good point. No probationer could realistically expect to take charge of a job with so little experience. I was in no position to make such big decisions, therefore I had no right to the pay linked with the additional responsibility. I consoled myself with the fact that while my peers were picking up their bigger pay packets and sailing through their much-practised exams, I was learning how to be a firefighter.

Twelve

It was a steep learning curve and I realised fairly quickly that being a firefighter involved a lot more than attending incidents. Adam impressed upon me the importance of spending down time with the lads. The job demands a strong, unbreakable bond. Relationships are forged in fires where lives hang in the balance, and at road traffic accidents where every second is critical. However, it's round the mess table where you learn of the person behind the uniform. Collectively cooking a meal, joking around the snooker table, and settling down for a film together shaped the camaraderie and created an atmosphere of belonging. Our lives depended on the skill and commitment of each watch member as well as a belief in each other that could not be feigned.

"It's a fucking dead end." James spat from behind the wheel.

Tensions were running high. We were proceeding to a confirmed Persons' reported. Control relayed that several calls had been received for the same incident. Two people were trapped inside a house. Their lives depended on the speed of our arrival.

We had been sent standby, temporarily covering another station's area when the call came in. With several ongoing incidents, resources were stretched. Another appliance had also been mobilised, but they would be at least five minutes behind us.

I was clutching the A-Z, directing James through a sequence of turns while the rest of the crew shouted out road names. We were in unfamiliar territory and needed everyone on board.

The dead-end traffic sign had rocketed the anxiety levels. We could not afford the time needed to turn the appliance round.

I held the map. The outcome was in my hands.

"It's ok. Carry straight on."

James did as I directed, but the situation didn't improve.

"Kate, there's no way through!"

The control room operator, desperately powerless, pleaded over the radio, "What is your ETA?"

My heart pummelled against my rib cage, the pages of the map stuck to my clammy hands. Intensity and uncertainty mixed with a sickening fear of an imminent loss of life and coagulated in the pit of my stomach.

"Keep going!" The words spilled out. I was screaming.

A rise of James' left eyebrow and an almost imperceptible shake of the head suggested it was against his better judgement, but the appliance continued at speed.

"The road bends round to the left." I took heart by the fact it did. "Then there's a turning to your right."

By now, the smoke was visible, a small crowd had gathered outside the building. Pockets of people were in tears, hugging each other close. Pained faces lifted in hope at our arrival. In truth, I was equally pleased to see them.

We jumped off, pulling the hose reel as we made our way to the door. The radiated heat reached us as we crouched down, fitting our masks and running through our safety checks. Breathing in and out—the set was working. Breaking the seal of the mask—the rush of air confirmed I had positive pressure. Replacing the seal, I held my breath—there were no leaks. Operating my supplementary air supply—it was working. I was good to go.

The pump whirred in the background. People were screaming. My heart felt like it was trying to escape the confines of my chest as adrenaline coursed through my veins. I needed to control it. An elevated breathing rate would cause my cylinder of compressed air to empty quicker.

The air was filled with shouting, pleading, crying. It merged with the noise of the appliance. The blue lights ticked over in their housing, casting a recurring blue shadow over the scene. The heat was uncomfortable, the smoke layer a foot from the floor. I exchanged a fleeting glance with Paul, my BA partner. A nod that said, 'Come on. We've got this,' before we entered the property on our hands and knees.

Inside the property, we entered another world. The only sound was that of my breath inside the mask and the ominous crackling of fire.

It was like looking through a letterbox, everything above my eyeline was an impregnable blanket of grey. My mask was pressed against the brown carpet and my heart pounded on the floor. A sofa sprawled out to my left, and further along the room I could make out the supports of a TV stand, then the chair legs of a dining set.

"I can't see them!" Paul was shouting at me.

We scrambled upright, sacrificing our vision for speed.

You could not enjoy a Person's Reported—frantic searching, hoping and praying that you find them before it became too late; checking every inch of a building because you don't want to leave anyone behind, but at the same time knowing that every second you spend rummaging a room could cost someone their life. I could never remember the fire of a Person's Reported. It was secondary to everything else, a distraction to the real task at hand. I remembered the furniture, the cushions, the cupboards and the wardrobes. I remembered the whistling noise of the breathing apparatus masks as my partner and I attempted to converse under extreme duress. And I remembered the precise moment I stumbled across a sprawled limb.

"I've found something!"

Paul joined me in a heartbeat. "They're both here, let's get them out."

The couple had collapsed in each other's arms. We often found casualties together. Imminent danger seems to provide a powerful magnetism to the ones we love.

Throwing off our tunics, we changed our cylinders at the side of the road. My body was working hard to reduce my core temperature and I savoured the cool night air alongside the feeling of accomplishment. Both occupants would make a full recovery.

The emotion when lives are saved is indescribable. The potent mix of intense pressure, followed by a flood of relief was intoxicating. It would be impossible to replicate the high felt at that moment.

Back at the station, the empty cylinders were recharged and our fire kit piled into the washing machines. My T-shirt was soaked in sweat, my hair stuck to my blackened face. I could taste smoke and I stunk of fire.

The post incident shower was always welcomed.

Soot poured off me as I appreciated the refreshing jet of hot water massaging my back. I was starting to relax, the intensity of the last hour was behind me. The adrenaline fuelled activity of life and death situations created a form of energy debt that needed to be repaid. The physical exertion and mental application involved in Person's Reported house fires required your body to go beyond what it was normally capable of and a period of recuperation was necessary.

CLUNK.

The emergency lights kicked in a fraction of a second before the call out tone reverberated around the station.

"Oh Shit!"

"Fuck."

The locker room air turned blue as clothing was scraped

on damp skin and we arrived at the fire appliance in several states of undress.

We were off again.

At training school, we were given three minutes to shower so I learned to be quick. Sophie and I resorted to a hair and body combo to minimise time and maximise cleanliness. However, after a swimming session at a local pool, we relished our instructor free moment and took the daring decision to apply not only shampoo, but conditioner as well. We came outside to find everyone waiting in the minibus and were lambasted on the side of the road for a good five minutes. It was some time before I conditioned my hair at work again.

A firefighter never knows what is around the corner. Adrenaline levels subside and peak as each shift ebbs and flows. As a probationer, I spent a large amount of time studying—every detail of equipment and operating procedures had to be committed to memory and I had to familiarise myself with the specific hazards and topography of my station area. However, at 22:00 hours on a nightshift, incidents depending, we would gather in the TV room for a film.

Distributing the cups of tea among the watch, I asked what everyone was watching.

"Rita, Sue and Bob too," replied one of the lads.

I took my seat. "Oh right, I haven't seen the first one."

The lads guffawed at my innocent remark and I nestled contentedly into my seat. I was blissfully happy. It was six months since I graduated from the training school and I felt as if I had found my spiritual home. I loved my job and the people I got to work with.

Thirteen

The sense of belonging to the brotherhood of firefighters intensified on a Tuesday dayshift in September 2001.

News of two aeroplanes hitting the World Trade Centre reached us as we cleaned lengths of hose in the yard.

We filed upstairs and stood in silence around the small TV in the canteen area. Mesmerised by the live pictures being broadcast, and acutely aware of the difficulties facing the emergency services, we became immersed in our own thoughts.

It was horrific. I could relate to the actions of the firefighters, but I could not comprehend the magnitude of their task. The tallest building that I had faced was a purpose-built block of flats that stood 15 floors high. The lifts could not accommodate all our personnel so the majority of us would run up the cramped stairwells burdened with equipment and the knowledge that lives depended on us getting there fast. 30 flights of stairs with full fire kit, breathing apparatus sets, lengths of hose and first aid equipment was exhausting. The firefighters entering the world trade centre were facing over 200 flights of stairs.

We watched as the emergency services herded scores of people through the exit. Lives were being saved, but the same camera shot also contained the haunting pictures of people falling to their deaths.

Then the towers came down.

We were speechless. Words were redundant as we each tried to process the catastrophic turn of events.

And then there was Adam.

"Right, well those jobs are not going to do themselves."

I looked across at him in disbelief: cleaning the appliances and putting out the rubbish could surely wait for one day. Adam had stood and made his way out the door. He was a one off. It did not matter what was going on in the rest of the world, the fire station was his empire and it would function as normal. I guess in a way, he mirrored the spirit of those at Ground Zero, life went on.

It would be some time before we discovered that 343 firefighters died at the twin towers that day, but we knew when the buildings collapsed there would have been significant numbers of emergency services still inside. The people in the planes and those at the higher floors of the tower had stood no chance of survival from the moment of impact.

We were on dayshift the following day and a decision was made for all firefighters at each station across the brigade to observe two minutes of silence. I thought it was too soon, too raw, but I also felt the overwhelming urge to do something. We stood to attention on the forecourt of the station, showing our respect to the people who never made it home. It was a sobering experience. As I stood shoulder to shoulder with my colleagues, the reality of our career choice hit home. Any given call could be our last. But I did not let the thought cloud my mind. Single minded focus was essential for a successful conclusion to an incident and the task in hand outweighed personal consideration.

Our station stood on a main road with a mini roundabout right outside, cars slowed to negotiate the hazard and catching sight of us, beeped their horns in solidarity. The two minutes passed in a cacophony of car horns. The fire service and the community united in our thoughts.

I had no idea that in 14 months' time the horns would sound again, but for very different reasons.

I barely had two years of service when the national firefighter strike took place in 2002. I was on a probationer's pay scale and would remain there for a further 20 months. The salary was not great. Sophie had taken a pay cut from her position as housing officer. I earned more than I did as a sports hall attendant, but after pension contributions, life insurance and union fees were deducted, I had less disposable income.

In 2002, the firefighters pay formula was linked to the upper quarter of industrial workers' wages. It was created after the last major fire service strikes of 1977 and 1978. A quarter of a century had passed and the industrial workforce had declined dramatically, while the demands placed on firefighters through expanded duties had risen.

I believed the outdated wage structure and the broadening of our responsibilities provided compelling reasons for increasing firefighters' wages. However, I was 24, single and happy with my contract. I had not forgotten my desire to join the job and the subsequent elation at being successful. Therefore, I could not get on board with a demand for higher pay without feeling hypocritical. The Fire Brigades Union were asking for a 40% rise. It was a preposterous figure, but it was designed to align firefighters pay with that of the police and that seemed entirely reasonable.

Furthermore, I could see the turmoil in the eyes of my workmates as the job they loved conflicted with a stable family life. They wanted a living wage, a pay that would allow them to spend their free time with their families instead of working in a taxi or up a ladder cleaning windows. We were by no means alone in our struggle—staff at seven UK airports, including Heathrow and Gatwick, were set to walk-out in a dispute over pay, Magistrates Courts were closed in an unprecedented strike and the postal workers' dispute rumbled on.

There was no sense of entitlement, nor an elevated perception of worth. Our grievance was born from frustration surrounding an antiquated pay formula, but it intensified when Tony Blair's Labour government announced that a pay increase for the fire service could only be funded by a change in working practices.

I had been a firefighter for long enough to realise that

our standard operating procedures existed for a reason. Lives depended on them. Consequently, I was fully behind the strike and walked out the doors with my brothers and sisters in November 2002.

We were slated by certain sections of the media. 'The Sun', amongst others, reported that the public had turned against us and offered us no support. Portrayed as selfish and greedy, we were putting lives in danger. At a time when our troops were needed elsewhere, we were reducing the number of frontline personnel by forcing them to staff the so-called 'Green Goddesses' (these green painted vehicles were built for the Auxiliary Fire Service, which disbanded in 1968. The self-propelled pumps were designed to pump huge quantities of water from rivers, lakes and other sources in the wake of a nuclear attack. They were a far cry from our modern, equipped for purpose, fire engines).

My own viewpoint, from the picket line on a freezing cold winter, was a stark contrast. We picketed 24 hours a day and the warmth shown by members of our community matched the heat of the brazier. People from all walks of life generously supported the picket lines. Taxi companies, fast food outlets, bakeries and other establishments would periodically deliver supplies. In the early hours of a particularly cold morning, an elderly woman dropped off some sandwiches and flasks of tea. This was our public. We would willingly risk our lives to save theirs and in those long, bitter nights, the kindness and support shown clearly indicated that the people who mattered most, appreciated us.

It was my first experience of picketing and I hated it despite the silver linings. Morale would be high at the start of a shift and the days were bearable. There was an abundance of food, company and amusing stories.

The evenings were punctuated by visitors, but the streets became deserted as the temperature dropped and ten of us would huddle around the brazier counting down the hours until the next watch took over at 09:00 hours.

Conversations became sporadic as late night turned into early morning. The dancing flames became hypnotic and silence fell across the group. James looked forlornly across the fire.

"I took wor lass shopping today."

He had our attention and our sympathy. Christmas was approaching, but there was not much money coming in.

"She wanted a pair of shoes, but I said no, not until this is sorted."

We all murmured in agreement.

Placing a protective arm around his shoulder, Adam consoled his senior firefighter, "She'll understand."

"That's what I thought, so later when we were tucked up in bed, I went to put my arm round her, you know…"

We nodded, rooting for him

"Well she sat up and said, 'Uh uh. If you do not shoe the horse, you do not ride the horse!'"

We all fell about laughing.

I love the ability many firefighters have of finding humour in any situation.

The need for 24-hour picketing was lost on me. I was on board with the cause and was willing to do whatever was necessary, but sitting freezing outside the station during the night seemed futile and detrimental to my health. I was so blind to any potential benefit of night picketing that I automatically believed my fellow workers felt the same. Therefore, when a vote was taken on the matter, I confidently raised my hand for the 'against' side.

Remarkably, only one other person raised their hand—an older guy with limited time left in the job, which people clearly expected. All eyes were on me. I hastily back tracked, pretended I misunderstood and quickly changed allegiance.

I instantly regretted my vote. It was a betrayal of our working union. I was motivated entirely by my own comfort, while they were driven exclusively by the cause.

However, my self-recrimination was unnecessary as a few weeks later common sense descended—it was decreed, presumably from the union, that midnight to 07:00 hours would be a no picketing period.

There were so many changes, so many strikes and last-minute cancellations of walkouts as negotiations stepped up, that it was difficult to keep track of time and events. I felt as if I was on a ride that I had no control over so I went along with the masses. I did what I was expected to do.

The decision to strike was not taken lightly and the withdrawal of labour was something we all struggled with. Firefighters were reluctant to remove support from their communities and decisions were made to respond to incidents where lives were at risk. However, there were still fatalities during the strike period. We care passionately about the people we serve and news of the casualties hit hard. The public deserved a first-class response and I viewed the strike as a necessary short-term action for a permanent solution. I was naïve and idealistic. I could not comprehend a world where saving lives was secondary to saving money, but there was a strategy in place and it was going to play out, regardless.

The dispute wrangled on for over eight months, but the strike finally fizzled out as a form of agreement was reached in the summer of 2003. The package involved substantial modernisation, which meant an overhaul of our working practices and job losses. It also included a cumulative 16% pay rise—4% was to be backdated to November 2002, 7% was to take effect from November 2003 and the remaining in July 2004.

The combined pay rise took a qualified firefighter's pay to £25,000 per annum, but it came at a price. The ensuing modernisation equated to cuts. The reductions introduced in the aftermath of the 2002/3 strike may have gone unnoticed by the public, but they have been felt deeply by our community as the number of firefighter deaths increased drastically. Fourteen firefighters lost their lives between 2003 and 2013, more than double the previous decade. Furthermore, in November 2015, FIRE magazine reported that the suicide rate amongst firefighters was a third higher than the national average.

It would be unjust to attribute these deaths to a single factor, but it is my belief that cuts have had an impact.

Fourteen

The service today is unrecognisable to the one that I joined. There have been numerous improvements to technology and our duties have expanded. The Fire service became the Fire and Rescue service as we took on a plethora of different incidents and trained for every eventuality. However, we have lost fire stations, fire engines and fire-fighters. Response times are increasing and resources are at breaking point.

Later arrival times reduce the possibility of saving a life. Every death is tortuous and self-persecution reigns. My mind replays these incidents in high definition and painful slow motion. Could I have put the fire out quicker? Found them sooner? We do not make the decisions, but we do have to live with the consequences. Longer response times may be a mere figure to most, but they are a heart-breaking reality for those in need of urgent help and we are left to bear witness to the lives destroyed.

The struggle threw everything off balance. I felt as if I was a pinball, bouncing around with no purpose other than to stay in the game. It was difficult to get a footing, a rhythm, or a period of relative normality. Intermittent strike action was finally behind us, but we were now facing station closures, removal of fire engines and job losses.

I found a safe haven with Russ and Paul who had joined the watch shortly after me. We were an unlikely trio—Russ had been a bank manager, was in his late thirties and lived in suburbia with his wife and two children; Paul had spent the last 15 years on the building sites, and his wife had recently given birth to twins so he now had four children under school age, but Paul was as relaxed as they came. I doubted our paths would ever have crossed in the outside world. However, we shared a sense of humour, an ideology and our probationary firefighters' journey. Put simply, we grew up in the fire service together.

Our contrasting personalities are perhaps best illustrated by our individual responses to Adam's routine and highly problematic question—"Would you like some more training?". You couldn't say 'No' without appearing cocky, and yet an answer in the affirmative had the potential to suggest our line manager's personally designed training schedule was lacking. I found safe ground by deviating from the routine drills and requesting familiarisation on specialist appliances or high-risk sites. I presented as showing an interest beyond my immediate environment, but in reality I enjoyed the excursions to the airport and the ride on the fire boat.

On that particular day, Russ's dark hair shook from side

to side, his eyes scrunched shut with self-recrimination as he came out of Adam's office. He towered above me as he spoke with his usual calm, even tone.

"I asked for more breathing apparatus drills."

I looked up at him in disbelief. His expression of confused acceptance was comical. "I know, I know." He held his arms up. "I just felt like I needed to say something and it was the first thing that came to my head!"

I found Russ' conscientiousness and diligence endearing and I smiled up at the guy who had inadvertently added to my workload.

And then there was Paul.

Paul was a qualified electrician and had spent years on various building sites, honing his piss-taking skills. When the Gaffer broached the subject of training with Paul, he unwittingly did so in front of an audience and Paul took centre stage.

"Ahhh never mind all that!" Paul waved a hand dismissively.

I quickly caught Russ' eye and then looked down, desperately suppressing the urge to laugh. Like the morbid draw of a car crash, I wanted to stare, but equally was afraid of what I might see.

"I've got a riddle for you," continued Paul. "What has seven eyes but cannot see?"

"Easy," the Gaffer's confidence permitted me to look up. "A potato!"

Adam smirked. Russ and I nodded. Paul shouted,

"WRONG! Three blind mice and half a sheep's head!"

Our superior shook his head, climbed out of his chair and left the room.

We waited until he was out of earshot before we collapsed in laughter.

Russ, Paul and I enjoyed a probation filled with drills and laughs. However, we were all seriously committed to our new careers and decided to take our Leading Firefighters exams. Much of the content overlapped our current studies and we thought it would prove useful in later years. Adam was categoric on his stance.

"You should be concentrating on becoming firefighters! I can't stop you entering the process, but I don't believe any of you have enough time-in to consider promotion. I won't support your application and I won't set aside any time to practice your drills."

The issue of time-in was becoming increasingly frustrating. Length of service was a badge of honour and widely regarded as equating to competence. I was in my third year and seeking qualifications to the rank of leading firefighter. Adam had achieved leading firefighter, sub officer and station officer within his first four years. I found his hypocrisy and dual standards infuriating.

Nevertheless, we were determined, and thanks to the other lads on the watch giving up their free time to help us, all three of us successfully passed both the practical and theoretical elements.

Despite the fact that everyone else on my recruits' course

had been deemed competent to act up, Adam decreed that I was not ready. I was confident that my nationally approved qualification would convince him otherwise.

As Adam distributed our certificates, I eagerly anticipated the prospect of acting up the next set.

I didn't, nor did I the set after that, and by the following set I had run out of patience.

I felt wronged and used my sense of injustice to summon up the courage to knock on Adam's door. After a few seconds, his voice allowed me to come in. I swallowed hard and entered.

The Gaffer lifted his head and peered at me through his spectacles, removing them as he addressed me by my name. I gave myself a moment. My heart was racing and I did not want my voice to break as I formed my argument.

"Gaffer."

He raised his eyebrows.

"I wanted to ask when I would be acting up."

He motioned me to sit, so I did.

"When I think that you are ready."

My heart rate quickened and the deep thuds acted as a call to action, my fists clenching in response. I could feel a tidal wave of anger rising through my chest. I gritted my teeth and contained the emotion. With enormous self-control, I argued,

"But I've passed an exam that states that I'm ready."

"Yes, the assessors have deemed you competent, but you're on my watch and therefore it's my responsibility to make sure you reach my standards and my requirements before I allow you to act up."

I could not speak. Anger and frustration were replaced by a feeling I had not encountered before. It took a few seconds to realise it was hopelessness. I felt empty and powerless. The course of my career appeared entirely out of my control. Furthermore, I felt responsible for Russ and Paul's subsequent lack of development—they were behind me in the queue. I desperately wanted to believe that Adam's idiosyncrasies were indiscriminate, but in my heart I knew that wasn't true—we had spent a substantial amount of time practising for both my friends' probationary assessments. However, I was in no position to argue.

Sophie had moved out in December 2001, but we saw each other regularly. I drank tea in her new home and updated her on the latest development. The strike had exasperated the financial strain I was feeling after taking over sole responsibility for the flat. The repercussions of Adam's decision went beyond my professional development.

"That's ridiculous." Sophie's frustration was palpable. Our watches could not have been more different. Her station was quieter and served a more affluent area. Her station officer seemed lovely, and the atmosphere appeared infinitely more laidback. They had affectionately nicknamed her 'Blister', jokingly suggesting that she popped up when the work was done. I could only imagine the ramifications if I had acquired a similar reputation.

Sophie spoke for us both, "I don't know what his

problem is!"

I was about to find out.

My watch sat in the lecture room on the blue clothed chunky chairs. The lectern was pushed to one side. This was an informal meeting with some union officials. They were regular visitors to the station after members voiced their discontent at the lack of communication. We felt we were being kept out of the loop, but in reality our leaders were just as uninformed.

They had concluded their update and we sat back in our seats, taking in the latest round of conjecture.

"Has anyone got anything else that they want to ask or get off their chests?" Rob, the branch secretary, stood and picked up his coat, but his tone was genuine and hopeful. Morale was low as modernisation was taking hold. We felt disconnected. Decisions that affected our safety and our ability to do our job were entirely out of our hands, but we were spent. The fight had been exhausting and we had failed. Stations were closing and jobs were lost. Rob was desperately searching for life—even anger was better than apathy.

"Actually, yes I do." All eyes turned to the Gaffer.

"I want to know why my son didn't pass the recruitment process."

I felt uncomfortable. Union officials have no say in the selection of firefighters. It was a strange forum for Adam to air his views.

"Well," Rob paused, now clearly wishing he hadn't asked. "Each stage is designed to test different things, he must know which bit he failed on?"

"He didn't even get past the application form!"

Rob sat back down, resigned to a conversation. "They're looking for certain words and phrases. He has to be able to show he can deal with a variety of different things. You know what I mean..."

"Apparently not! I did his form for him!" Despite himself, Adam smiled.

James seized on this information and launched into a light-hearted assault on the Gaffer. He took it for a few seconds before firing back.

"The whole thing is ridiculous. Everyone knows that Firefighters should be male, white and heterosexual!"

I glared at him in shock, astounded by his candour and half expecting him to laugh. But Adam continued.

"They should have a 42-inch expansion chest, a crew cut, be between 5 foot 10 and 6 foot 2, and be a time served tradesman."

Silence descended and the jovial atmosphere turned thick. I looked down, reluctant to catch anyone's eye. I willed the ground to swallow me up.

"These are your thoughts, Adam, and you are entitled to them, but you cannot speak for everyone. Personally, I feel we have a stronger, more efficient workforce now we have diversified."

It was a professional response from an official, but his crimson face suggested it was also a desperate salvage mission.

"I think we will have to agree to disagree." Adam left the room and the atmosphere lifted slightly.

I looked around the room. We were all ruled out by Adam's comment. Some were closer than others, but whether it was an inch or a banking background, none of us made Adam's firefighter grade. However, it was painfully obvious that I was the furthest removed. It was a sucker punch, winding my pride. Any notion I had that I was a welcome addition to Adam's team was knocked out of me.

Adam's speech came out of the blue, but practically every firefighter knew a deserving applicant who had been unsuccessful in the selection process. Blame was apportioned to the government targets and questions began to surface as to whether the best candidates were being recruited. In reality, the publication of those figures did little to boost recruitment. In 2006, the female contingent made up just 3% of the total workforce, and by the time London hosted the 2012 Olympic Games it had increased to a mere 4%. It seemed that this derisory increase came at the expense of the reputation of female firefighters.

Unfortunately, as our numbers expanded there were some who seemed to confirm this bias. Refusing to wash up was a controversial contention of gender bias; negating senior orders on the grounds of presumably knowing better; unsubstantiated claims of bullying and harassment and sitting on a wall while colleagues grafted because it was their time of the month—all contributed to a myriad of further stories and embellishments which tarnished female firefighters with the same suspicion. How many of these were true or embellished was hard for me to make out, but the others took at face value.

Adam was one of the longest serving station officers in the country. I strongly believed that any breakdown to our working relationship would be attributed to me. Reluctant to add more fuel to the fire, I kept quiet, but it was a low point for me.

I had kept my head down, worked tirelessly and did everything that was asked of me, but I had been judged on characteristics entirely outside my control. I thought back on the past four years—despite coming in on my day off, I had not been given any time to practice for my probationary exams. It suddenly occurred to me that I was being set up to fail. It also threw a fresh perspective on Adam's refusal to allow me to 'act up'. The recruitment banner that adorned the front of the station sickened me. 'Fire does not discriminate and neither do we!' was a devastating misrepresentation of my reality.

Fifteen

I was left reeling from Adam's disclosure, so when the opportunity presented itself, I enjoyed a six-week distraction working for major league soccer camps in Denver, Colorado. I blocked my annual leave entitlement together and the Gaffer granted the necessary permission.

I returned with a swell of self-belief and initiated a transfer request. Adam called me into his office.

"I hear you want to leave. Can I ask why?"

I looked at my Gaffer. We shared no common ground; our backgrounds were polar opposites and our belief systems clashed. He looked affronted and I didn't know where to begin.

"Honestly?"

Adam nodded. His request was sincere.

"I don't think you want me here."

Adam's face crumpled in disbelief. Visibly shocked, he took off his glasses and pressed his fingers into his eyes. "So, you're telling me that you've put a transfer in because you think I don't want you here?"

"Yes. But, don't worry. I won't mention it."

It was the first time in our whole working relationship when I felt like Adam and I were actually having a conversation, and I felt strangely empowered by my shift in status.

Adam put his glasses on the table and turned to me, his expression serious and genuine.

"Kate, I'm sorry you've got that impression. I do want you here. I think you've settled in well and are a good addition to the watch. I would ask that you reconsider your transfer and finish your probation on this watch."

That should have been enough, it was all I had wanted, but it had taken too long. My time in the States had granted me the opportunity to rediscover myself. I was capable, confident, strong and happy. I should feel like that at work. I thanked Adam, but I was still determined to move on. However, in the next few hours, several senior officers visited our station and I was summoned to speak with them all. They each wanted to know what my problem was with Adam. I wasn't there to make a stand, I definitely didn't want to make a fuss, I just wanted to enjoy going to work. Yet, the reaction to my innocent request was intimidating and blame was gently guided to me as I was told I had misunderstood. I had inadvertently come up against the weight of the brigade and by lunchtime, I had withdrawn my request. That day still proved to be a turning point for me. Adam and I had a better understanding of each other, the lines of communication opened up and he immediately allowed me to 'act up'. I felt like I was finally making progress in my career.

During my four years serving under Adam, I accelerated up the ranks of responsibility as my watch underwent something of a metamorphosis. Several of my original colleagues had gained promotion, we had a surge of new recruits and were left very short on drivers.

Adam summoned me to his office where I was asked to attend the driving course. It was an unexpected, but appreciated sign of approval. However, I had only held my car licence for 12 months, so given my lack of experience both in terms of fire-fighting and driving, I respectfully declined the Gaffer's invitation.

It transpired that it was not an invitation, but an order. The Gaffer humoured me and said he understood my concerns, but the waiting list was so long, it would be at least a year before I would obtain a place on the course.

Adam's estimations were remarkably inaccurate. I received an invitation for an LGV medical the very next set and had a starting date within a month.

I got to grips with the size and weight of the appliance fairly quickly; however, I struggled with the reversing element and was nervous on the morning of the exam.

My career would not be affected by the result, nor would my standing as a firefighter, but I was keen to avoid excessive ribbing from the lads. I loved the banter on the watch, it was entirely good humoured and never felt like a personal attack. It was the firefighters' way of making you feel included and I welcomed it.

Ribbing was one thing, but failure was another. I did

not want to let myself down nor did I want to disappoint my squad. I was representing my watch and I desperately wanted to make the grade.

The test began with the reversing element and I was pleased to get the chicane of cones out of the way. The emergency stop was next—careering across the yard at speed before ramming on the breaks as soon as the front wheels passed the flag. Then it was time to go out on the road. The drive allowed my examiner to judge how well I handled the appliance under normal driving conditions. Faulty temporary lights meant I spent a large portion of my exam in a traffic jam and I returned to my watch triumphant.

The assessment allowed me to drive a fire appliance, but not to an emergency. I had to accrue 20 hours of driving time before I could do the blue light training. So, I drove back from incidents and chauffeured for hydrant inspections and any other routine work. Although the vast majority of these 20 hours were accumulated driving the second appliance, I did drive the Gaffer on several occasions. To me, this revealed significant progress in our working relationship.

By Christmas 2004, I had officially completed my probationary period and enjoyed the status of qualified firefighter. It came with the additional benefit of an increase in pay and I felt like an equal among my male counterparts.

I was only four weeks away from becoming a qualified Emergency Fire Appliance Driver (EFAD) when another recruit joined our watch. I was perversely fascinated but overwhelming fearful when Bridget walked through the station door.

"You can discuss shades of lippy and all that!" The lads assumed I would be pleased.

I laughed, but I was wary of becoming too friendly with our latest new recruit. I did not want to create a gender divide and in truth I had succumbed to Adam's projected prejudices. The term 'female firefighter' was now laced with negative connotations. I wanted to be a firefighter without any additional labels or special considerations.

It was not the name her mother gave her, but Bridget was short, and the lads thought it was funny to rhyme her name with this trait. All restrictions had been lifted with regards to age, height and weight. It was no longer a matter of finding the person for the job. It was now a case of making the equipment fit the person.

I desperately wanted Bridget to succeed in winning the Gaffer round. I offered advice and encouragement, but I refused to get too involved. I had fought hard to attain a tenuous vein of respect from the man in charge and was reluctant to jeopardise it.

I had spent four years doggedly proving my worth. I made sure I was the last person back to the appliance after a job, I always chose to carry the heavier items of equipment and I volunteered for the industrious yet tedious roles that nobody wanted. Despite the Gaffer's stance on female fire-fighters, I gave him very little cause for complaint. He once told me to spend less time studying to allow more time with the lads and there was a fallout after I 'only' got 80% for a probationary assessment (in truth my entire course scored the same mark—a lack of instructors led to an agreement of a blanket score of 4 out of 5, unless anyone did anything stupid). On balance, I felt that I had done everything possible to improve the reputation of women in the job.

I passed the baton to Bridget and attended my blue light driving course at the brigade headquarters. It was there that I was told Adam had left his position with immediate effect.

I phoned the station and Russ described the circumstances surrounding Adam's impromptu move.

"Kate man, you should have seen it. We were wearing BA on the third floor of the drill tower and Bridget started crawling along the balcony on all fours!"

"What?!"

The concrete training tower had five floors, each enveloped by a three-foot high balcony. The ladder was pitched to the sill. It was standard practice to maintain a grip on the ladder and step down onto the safety of the floor. Bridget's decision to remain on the precipice was beyond ludicrous.

"Adam was screaming at her. Then he got Paul to demonstrate, but she said she needed a step. Adam said he had seen enough, stormed inside, and the next thing we knew he left!"

Adam's sudden departure was unexpected, but I couldn't honestly say I was sorry. I was looking forward to working under a new manager, someone who would hopefully hold different views on what makes an ideal firefighter.

Whatever I thought of Adam, he was honest and straight talking and I respected him. He demanded high standards and led by example. He was also my only station officer. Roles were soon introduced to replace the rank structure and station officers became watch managers. Adam was the first and last person I called Gaffer.

Sixteen

"The whole is greater than the sum of its parts."
Aristotle

A fire service watch is the best example I have seen of synergy in action. Football manager, Alex Ferguson, famously singled out the V formation of migrating geese to be the ultimate paradigm in teamwork. I would not disagree, but in human form, I believe a watch would take some surpassing.

Every watch is different. They are all comprised of unique characters from diverse backgrounds and each individual contributes something personal to the overall team dynamic and ultimately to its success. It could be the calm, commanding voice of the watch manager; the driver who knows every shortcut; the authority on specialist incidents; the electrician who can rectify a fault unknown to their colleagues; or the probationer whose infectious enthusiasm is extremely welcome during long nights of rubbish fires and false alarms. Everyone plays their part.

I'm naturally positive and don't take myself too seriously,

but I believe my greatest contribution to the fire service has been my individuality. The diversification of a workforce reaches far beyond the inclusion of minority members. It is about allowing every person to be themselves. We each have unique qualities to contribute, but if we indulge our natural reluctance to stand out, we risk settling for a comfortable collective mediocrity. Incessant banter and put downs are integral aspects of life as a firefighter; 'fucking dickhead', 'prize nob' and 'wanker' are among the most popular ways to address your mates. It's light-hearted, good natured and by no means malicious. However, despite extreme temptation at times, I can never bring myself to insult someone. Consequently, I became a confidant, trusted with secrets that the lads would not share with each other. Uniquely privy to their vulnerabilities and concerns, I could steer conversations beyond the usual topics of football, beer, women and cars.

"You see, what people don't realise is, as long as the ground is dry, your washing will dry." Russ eagerly demonstrated his domestic knowledge and nodded in my direction as Paul entered the locker room. I had become a convenient excuse for non-macho discussions.

Soaps started figuring in the evening viewing to the tune of, "Kate wanted this on," even if I don't watch soaps.

Male, white, heterosexual men form the heart of the workforce and ultimately wield the overwhelming power to initiate change. It was a slow and subtle transition, but as barriers of pretence were broken down, people could finally be who they wanted to be.

After Adam's sudden departure, I felt like a fish that had survived a drought. I'd been getting by and now I believed I would thrive. However, things didn't turn out as I expected.

Adam's successor was in place within a week of his departure. Nathan was in his mid-forties, stocky and clean shaven with dark hair. He did not share Adam's beliefs on the ideal firefighter. Black or white, male or female, gay or straight, Nathan did not care. He appeared to hold every firefighter in equal contempt.

Nathan was by no means an ogre, but he had been given an unfeasibly difficult task. As a temporary watch manager, his performance would be scrutinised by his superiors and his future prospects determined by his results. It was a difficult period with a great deal of uncertainty. Morale was low as the strike burned out and cuts took effect. It could not have been a good time to stamp your authority.

In addition, Nathan inherited a watch who had only known one gaffer, including James who had twenty years in the job. Subsequently, there was a period of adjustment as we learned to accommodate our new manager. Adam had encouraged us to think for ourselves and had created a definite division between himself and the watch, whereas Nathan dictated our every move and wanted to be one of the lads. He was generous with his time and would be the first to buy anyone a drink. I appreciated his enthusiasm and his willingness to engage with his team. However, he also had a vicious temper. There were never any warnings or red flags. You never knew which Nathan would turn up. It made things difficult as the lines became blurred—one minute we would be sharing a joke with our officer in charge and a second later we would be on the wrong end of an ear bashing. Life in the mess room swayed from joviality to anger and I did not like the constant threat of imminent tension.

I found myself yearning for the steadfast disapproval of Nathan's predecessor. Adam's departure had serious consequences.

The abrupt end to his twenty-seven-year reign was cloaked in speculation. The fact it coincided with Bridget's arrival brought widespread notoriety to female firefighters.

I've always had a need to be useful and to prove my worth. Perhaps it stems from playing with older children on the estate in Bishop Auckland, or from competing alongside the boys at football. If I could not compete physically, I used technique, and if I was lacking technically, I would make up for it in effort. There was always something I could do.

That's how I approached my position as a firefighter. I felt as if I had something to prove and I carried the assumption that Adam's views were representative of the majority of the workforce. The competence of firefighters was widely implied by their gender—males were proficient, whereas women were not and it was infinitely more difficult to disprove a theory than accept the status quo.

While I had spent my late teens and early twenties having a

laugh, my early years in the fire service forced me to grow up. I was an entirely different person at work. I felt stressed, suffocated and scrutinised, and I didn't want that version of myself to seep into my personal life, not least because I had started to see someone. I purchased my flat under the council's right-to-buy scheme and was suddenly confronted with responsibility from all angles. I had gone from a carefree young woman to a partner, a homeowner and a firefighter whose appointment was constantly challenged.

My career was dependent on my ability to consistently conform to the expectations of others. The structure of a uniformed service can be smothering. Every piece of information came from my immediate environment and I believed that what I was told carried the weight of the entire organisation. Female's had to prove themselves. Yet there was no pre-determined set of standards. Instead, my competence was entirely dependent on how others viewed me.

Dom had married, Liz had moved to Southport and Bernard was working split shifts as a chef. My parents were both working full time and although we all kept in touch over the phone, visits were infrequent. My friends didn't understand my career and although my work mates were supportive, I didn't feel I could discuss my vulnerability with them without confirming suspicions that women were weak. Sophie was now in a serious relationship and it became harder to meet up around our shifts. It was my problem and I had to deal with it.

Outside of work I was spending most of my spare time

with my girlfriend and football team. We were all of a similar age and ilk, and Sunday afternoon matches were followed by nights at the pub.

It was through football that I first became aware of confirmation bias. I captained the team and habitually played the full 90 minutes in centre midfield. I could make several bad passes and miss vital tackles with very little comeback as my reputation had been established. However, our left back played every game on borrowed time. She could play a blinder for 70 minutes, make one mistake, and be hauled off as the manager saw what he expected to see.

I recognised myself in our left back because it was how I suffered at work. I constantly felt as if I was one mistake away from failure and marginalisation in the Fire Service. I valued having a voice at football and if I felt any of the lasses were unfairly treated, I fought on their behalf.

We were making our way back onto the pitch after a tense half time talk when a team-mate caught up with me.

"You were right what you said in there."

I looked at her. "So, how come you didn't say anything?"

"Well, he kind of shot you down so I didn't see the point."

That was the problem. People would complain, but very few would take their argument forward. I couldn't understand that—it frustrated and angered me. I was further aggravated by my own sense of inadequacy. I wanted to help, but couldn't fight on someone else's behalf. I learned to let go of the things I had no control over. It was a timely reminder that I needed to focus on my own career.

I had carved out a niche for myself and I was fortunate that my watch supported me. I was confident in my abilities and comfortable with my place in the team. I knew that they had my back.

Unfortunately for Bridget, she was new and exposed. Her fight for acceptance was further hampered by the stowage of the lockers, as much of the equipment was outside of her reach.

A cheap, blue, plastic, foldaway step was expedited to our station and seemingly considered reasonable adjustment. It was an embarrassment for all concerned. It highlighted a complete lack of operational consideration from the upper echelons of the brigade—we were rarely afforded the luxury of time and the driver could not be expected to source a completely flat work surface. It also drew additional unwanted and unnecessary attention to Bridget. The step emphasised a problem without offering a credible solution. In time, the lockers would be modified to allow easier access, but for Bridget it was too little too late. Height is not something that a person can change. Bridget had passed the selection process and was offered a position as a firefighter; if the working conditions were incompatible with her stature, then the fault lay with the brigade, not Bridget.

The excessive scrutiny knocked Bridget's confidence. Perhaps aware that every mistake would be magnified and used against her, she chose to do very little.

At first, we didn't notice. Then when we did, it became a joke and the lads christened her B.I. Jane. Bone Idle for short. But increasingly it became irksome to those of us picking up the slack. Senior hands would take regular trips down nostalgia lane and conclude,

"You wouldn't have gotten away with it in my day."

It was incontrovertible. However, the tag line was unmerited.

"We didn't have female firefighters then."

It was unfair and infuriating, but the ludicrous generalisation effectively obliterated my efforts over the previous four years. I was disillusioned and I hated the fact that my prospects were hopelessly out of my control. The strength, resilience and determination I had shown throughout my career were soon forgotten. The new blanket expectation was that female firefighters were inherently lazy and inept.

I was angry, powerless and increasingly frustrated. My gender was underestimated while there were men such as Rick, who fabricated details about his life and took little responsibility in his work. Although I noticed it, I chose not to say anything, knowing this would not make a difference and people would see through him in the end. They did, and he lost the trust of the watch. He moved to a station in Sunderland, but there was never a suggestion that every male firefighter should now be likened to him.

Regrettably, I kept my distance and did little to help Bridget's cause. I wanted to be a firefighter without the need for a prefix and I needed to preserve my own reputation.

Ultimately, Bridget was reassigned to another role within the brigade. Her physical presence on our watch was almost negligible as her brief time as an operational fire-fighter coincided with a turbulent time in my private life.

At the turn of 2005, my Grandma was given three months to live. In the end, I would only see the much-loved matriarch of our family a dozen more times.

"I would have liked to have learned to ride a bike," she mused, "but I'm not going to do that now, so... I have no regrets."

My Grandma's strength, humour and faith remained throughout her final few weeks, and continues to have a profound effect on my life. In my ever-changing world, she was a constant, a rock of support and a comforting symbolic reminder of the infinite power of unconditional love. I felt an overwhelming peace in her presence.

Sadly, during the course of my Grandma's illness, my two-year relationship became strained and my partner moved on. I couldn't blame her. I valued our time together and she knew very little of my life at work. She had met the watch several times and I was happy for my personal and work life to mix, but I kept the details to myself. We shared some holidays with mutual friends and were involved with the same football team, but more often than not we went to the pub. I probably drank more than was healthy—it was a throwback to my student days, I wanted to live in the moment and free myself of any sense of responsibility. At the same time I was in almost constant pain with a shoulder injury, and I spent a ridiculous amount of time trying to hide it. A relationship requires investment from both sides and I was only willing to share certain aspects of my life. There was no bad feeling and she remains one of my closest friends.

At the time, I was too focused on my family to process the turmoil, but after my Grandma passed away, a huge chasm opened up in my life. Reality crashed down as I attempted to make sense of my new existence. One without my Grandma, my partner and my best friend. Sophie had taken an inter-brigade transfer and moved to Brighton with her girlfriend. It was a 6-hour drive away and it felt like the other side of the world. I had been in denial about her move until the day she left.

Sophie had transferred jobs, sold her home and made all the provisions to leave. I didn't want to believe it, but it was happening. For the first time in my life I felt lonely and vulnerable. My supportive bubble had burst, exposing me to a vacuum that I was desperate to fill. I was looking for a purpose rather than a person and I became restless. Desperate to do something, I signed up for the Edinburgh marathon, immersed myself in training and clung to work.

Seventeen

The fire service was both a reassuring anchor and a welcome distraction. I was pleased to have the driving to concentrate on.

My first shift as an emergency fire appliance driver was during a beautiful summer evening. It was the kind of night we would expect to be busy with small fires. Local youths were likely to be out and about, and wheelie bins, skips and cars would be an easy target for any budding arsonist. Fires with no life risk would be an ideal baptism for my fledgling driving career. I carried out the routine checks—all the lights were in working order, the oil, water and derv levels were above three quarters, the tyre pressures and tread depths were recorded.

Paul and James had adorned neck collars and strapped themselves down in the back. The incessant mickey taking was strangely reassuring. I was ready.

And I didn't have to wait long. The bells went down and the turn out system sprung into life. This was it.

I jumped in and waited for the station doors to open.

Seatbelt on, I started the engine and turned on the lights. My crew manager climbed on board and read out the turn out sheet: "Person on Fire. Park Road."

A Persons' reported heightens your senses. Every second and action counts. I have been to countless incidents where it has been confirmed that people are still inside the property. However, throughout my fire service career, I have only had two 'persons on fire'. That was the first, five minutes into my first shift as a fire appliance driver.

It was inexplicable and terrifying how quickly everything I ever knew was eradicated from my memory. In the rear cab, my topography had been excellent. Park Road was a main street and a road we used often to access many of our high-rise flats. But, in that moment, sitting behind the wheel, knowing the person was already likely to be in a bad way, I had absolutely no idea how to get there.

James shouted through from the back, "You know that one, yeah?"

"No. I can't think where it is." My mouth went dry, I could feel the perspiration on the steering wheel. I gripped it tighter. My heart was pumping fast, but it felt like the blood was bypassing my brain. The door was halfway up and I needed to know exactly where I was going in the next three seconds.

James' tone was as calm as ever, "Go right down West Road, then…"

He never got a chance to finish. The door was almost up and every road name I had ever learned had gone. I needed to tell him straight.

"James seriously, I don't even know where West Road is."

The fact our station was on West Road told James all he needed to know, but I made it crystal clear: "Please just tell me left or right!"

The door was up, we were away. I focused on getting through the traffic as James directed. We arrived at the scene in less than two minutes. Unfortunately, the homeless man had succeeded in taking his own life. There was nothing we could do.

That was my first and most stressful blue light drive. The life risk was compounded by the fact that my memory appeared to shut down. I had come to know our station area extremely well, but it all counted for nothing when I was actually asked to drive.

There are a lot of things to consider when you're driving a fire engine. You have to take responsibility for your own driving and make allowances for random manoeuvres performed by members of the public. There's an enormous amount of pressure when you think that someone's chance of survival depends largely on the time it takes for you to get that appliance and the crew to them. It's not uncommon for new drivers to forget routes that have previously been ingrained.

After my initial 999 drive, things got easier. The worst scenario had already happened and the majority of the incidents that followed were less daunting in comparison. My local knowledge came back to me and I no longer needed to rely on information coming from the back seat. I was largely enjoying the whole experience.

I was also relishing my independence.

Clear of student debts and the limiting factors of an incompatible relationship, I nurtured my own interests and decided to learn to surf. My friends lacked either the leave, the funds, or the inclination to do it with me. A week surfing in Fuerteventura was my first solo holiday, and it gave me so much more than tuition. My sense of freedom and confidence grew, and I returned with lifelong friends and a renewed determination to live life to the fullest, as my grandmother had.

The rumpus surrounding Bridget had passed and I was becoming more accustomed to Nathan's moods. In fact, his flare ups usually had an unintentional comical effect, and as such lost their impact. Furthermore, the fact that I was now a driver increased my contribution to the watch.

I loved driving the fire engines, especially if the job turned out to be a false alarm or a smaller fire. Driving to the limit of the appliance is a huge adrenalin rush. However, I spent the bulk of my driving career covering the city centre. The mass of the fire engine eliminates any opportunity to zip through traffic. Every decision is a careful consideration of risk. Speed is necessary, but should never be used at the expense of safety. Commonly, a careful negotiation of a clear path is all that is required, but a Persons' reported incident will demand a drive at the uppermost threshold of both the driver's and the appliance's capabilities.

The air is always charged when we are proceeding to a life risk, and dialogue is minimal. Each member of the crew goes about their role with maximum efficiency and remains completely focused on their specific task. The driver will take more calculated risks. The breathing apparatus wearers will get ready, with sets on and any necessary equipment to hand.

The first few minutes are intensely hectic: the breathing apparatus wearers in the back are starting up, ready to enter the property, while the watch manager is swallowed up in health and safety, desperately gleaning as much information as possible in order to put a rescue plan into operation.

That leaves the driver with everything else: running out hose, helping the breathing apparatus wearers with various equipment, locating a hydrant to ensure a decent water supply, setting up the breathing apparatus board to safeguard the wearers, lighting, fielding messages from the watch manager and our control staff, and if need be, requesting more appliances, an ambulance or assistance from the police.

Every single job is essential and requires completing immediately if not before.

In the midst of this, it would often take several attempts to find a working hydrant. Early on in my career, we would test every single hydrant to guarantee it was operating effectively. Decisions taken elsewhere dictated that practice was no longer considered necessary. I cannot adequately describe the sheer relief of finding a hydrant, knowing your friends are inside and entirely dependent on the supply of water, followed by the utter exasperation of realising it is defective.

Anything that's required to be done outside of the property is largely the responsibility of the designated driver, especially at the initial stages. Unfortunately, security of the appliance is another task that requires attention. Equipment does get stolen, and accountability lies with the driver.

This initial storm of frenzied activity is followed by an agonising wait of doing very little.

Once the water supply is established and the required pressure obtained, it takes very little to maintain it. At protracted incidents, the officer in charge may only need to pass a message to control every fifteen minutes. The lion's share of the work is carried out inside, and the driver is stuck with the appliance.

There are occasions, however, when the drivers have their own tribulations to deal with.

It was the very early hours of the morning and I was driving our first appliance, code name 'B01', to a persons' reported flat fire.

It was on the 14th floor and immediately visible as we left the station. Flames leapt from the window, garnishing the night sky with a belch from hell.

I prayed that the reports were wrong, as anyone who was in there stood very little chance of surviving. As soon as I pulled the appliance up, the lads jumped off. Both crews were already donned in breathing apparatus and heavily laden with various bits of equipment. Anything that might be required had to be taken up. At high rise fires, there's no time to come back to the appliance for any bit of kit.

Each block of flats over twelve metres high are fitted with a riser, essentially a tube that runs the height of the building. An inlet at the bottom can be plugged into with the water carried on the appliance. Each floor has an outlet that operates as a tap. The crews inside will plug their hose into the outlet and subsequently have water on the relevant floor.

I opened the riser inlet and ran out a length of hose from the appliance to charge the riser. The instant that I opened my tank, I realised there was a problem. The chamber emptied in seconds. It should have lasted at least two minutes, which would have provided me with a short, but workable amount of time to locate a hydrant and augment the supply.

Nathan was screaming for more water. James was driving the second appliance and had plugged in a length of hose from his appliance into the back of mine. It was a quick fix method to buy more time to find a hydrant. However, the same thing happened. We had emptied two fire engine tanks of water in less than thirty seconds.

The only explanation was that an outlet had been opened on at least one other floor; someone had tampered with life-saving equipment, and as a result the floors were flooding and preventing a decent water supply reaching the fire floor. A third pump had arrived from a neighbouring station. Personnel were scrambled to locate and close down the offending outlets and we used a third tank of water before we could get the hydrant in. We were able to maintain water on the fire floor, but not a sufficient pressure to allow any indent to be made on the fire.

Finally, all other outlets were closed down and progress could be made.

While James and I waited outside, fourteen floors above us the lads were trying desperately to force down doors. There was no chance of anyone surviving those conditions. I anxiously waited for the code implying a fatality to be passed. Eventually the radio crackled back into life.

"Bravo zero one," called Nathan.

"Bravo zero one, go ahead." I waited and involuntarily held my breath. This feeling was horrible, but I knew it was much worse for the lads who had discovered the body.

"There's nobody here. The flat is empty."

I exhaled. "Nice one!"

But Nathan quickly dampened my relief, "No, the doors were bolted from the inside…" Nathan was still talking, but I had stopped listening. I looked up fourteen floors and knew what he was going to ask. The occupier must have jumped.

"Okay, I'll check it out."

I grabbed a torch and a thermal image camera and went past James. He had heard the conversation over the radio and, sensing I would not be eager to fulfil my assigned task, volunteered to go on my behalf.

Some jobs appear more suited to a particular gender.

Heavy work is stereotypically a male dominated field, whereas females in general have a caring, nurturing nature which sees them make up a larger proportion of nurses and primary school teachers. Looking in the pitch black for the remains of someone that has fallen 150 feet is not particularly suited to either sex.

The task had been given to me, therefore I would do it. I was terrified, but I resolved not to show it. The need to prove myself had not subsided. I constantly felt as if I was on a precipice—one wrong move would leave my reputation, and subsequently my career, in tatters. Failing as a firefighter was my ultimate fear and I used it to overcome trepidation in all areas of my life. I vividly remember the first time I strapped a snowboard to my feet. I hesitated only a fraction of a second before launching myself down the slope. I feigned courage to my friends and favoured potential broken bones rather than exposing a personality flaw that could negatively reflect my suitability as a firefighter. In my late-twenties, I had not yet grasped the true meaning of bravery.

In the same vein, I set off to look for a body in the dead of night.

The immediate area was generally well lit. The appliances were on the main road and were further illuminated by the street lights. I advanced round that side of the block first. I came to the main entrance and the area directly around it was totally clear. As access and egress to the flats were via this section, the grass had been recently cut. I could make out that whole side of the building. It was completely clear.

No bushes, no hidden spots. This did not require further investigation.

I rounded the corner.

This side of the building did not benefit from any exterior lighting. It was enveloped in darkness and littered with thick bushes. I shone my torch over the area, but, as expected, could not see anything.

The affected flat was a corner apartment. It overlooked this side of the building, but also the opposite corner to which I stood. I searched the area briefly. It was futile in terms of the search, but it allowed my eyes to adjust and my brain to process what I was likely to encounter.

Looking for something you do not want to find is a strange experience. Our job brings us into contact with death and it's something we have to deal and reconcile with. Maybe some people do become used to it, but I never have and I doubt I ever will.

The ground directly under the flat was clearly a more plausible landing spot. So, I inched my way round and concentrated my efforts on that area. I was checking every step, shining the torch and scrutinising the thermal image camera, which detects heat. It was getting colder. And a body, even one recently deceased, would retain enough heat to show as a white glow on the screen.

Nothing showed. I looked everywhere, but eventually re-joined James at the appliances. I radioed through to Nathan, "Firefighter Fullen to watch manager."

"Go ahead." His reply was instant, as he had been

waiting for news.

"I've looked. There's nothing here."

Nathan was perplexed. The locks had all been bolted from the inside. They had searched every inch of the flat. It was empty.

At times like this I doubted myself. I knew I had searched every inch of the perimeter, but I also knew that the lads would be adamant that they had done the same. The fire had been extinguished, the smoke had cleared and there were at least 6 firefighters in a 1-bedroom flat. When it came down to it, it was more likely that I had missed a body in the pitch black, thick undergrowth.

Nathan ordered the firefighters on the 14th floor to return and drop off their sets before assisting with the search. A dozen pairs of eyes were dispatched, armed with thermal cameras and lighting to search the area.

Dawn was on the horizon, when Nathan finally concluded that no-one had jumped and nobody was to be found. I never went into the flat, but the lads that did were insistent that the bolts were on and furniture had been placed in front of the door. Both would be very strong indicators that someone was inside and it appeared that someone had wanted to make it look like that was the case. The mystery was not ours to solve. Our responsibility was the fire and it had been extinguished. There was no immediate danger to any of the flats' occupants, so nothing was left for us to do except make up our equipment and return to the station..

Return journeys are generally animated and a time

when the crew piece together the incident from each other's perspective. That period of time that stretches into the mess room and continues over a cup of tea is among my favourite moments in the fire service.

We never found out what happened in the flat that night, just as we never knew if critical casualties made it. Partial pictures can be difficult, but the lines of responsibility are clear. The Police and Ambulance Service are experts in their field and we must handover when our remit is complete. We talk things over on our watch and usually reach our own conclusion, but despite several attempts we found no credible answer to that particular mystery.

Eighteen

At incidents, drivers are the first to deal with any casualties. If an ambulance is delayed, the driver will generally be the one required to administer first aid until the paramedics or other professionals arrive.

In many circumstances, those who have lost consciousness are easier to deal with. Conscious casualties can be unpredictable. However, they can also be life savers.

At 4am, our second nightshift of a busy set, we got the call of confirmed Persons' reported. We were tired, temperatures had plummeted and it was a freezing cold January morning, but none of that mattered.

I was driving. The access was awkward, the street was split three ways and segregated by bollards. It was difficult to determine the best possible route, so we split the attendance to ensure one pump arrived in optimum time. We arrived first, but only by seconds. Practically everyone slipped on the ice in our eagerness to get the hose reel off.

The crew manager made light work of the door, and breathing apparatus teams poured into the building. Within seconds, a male casualty was brought out, clearly suffering from smoke inhalation. He was in desperate need of oxygen and was passed to me for treatment.

However, soon after hitting the fresh air, he regained consciousness and made several desperate attempts to charge back into the house.

It was by no means unusual. People go to extraordinary lengths to protect their loved ones. He had a height and weight advantage, but he had taken in a lot of smoke and after his first few struggles, it became clear the effort had taken its toll. I held him against a wall and tried to reason with him, but he was adamant that two other people were still inside.

A further male casualty was rescued. He was able to walk, aided by a BA crew, and was immediately passed on to the paramedics. Although there was no dialogue between the occupants, the relief on my charge's face on seeing his mate was palpable. It was the perfect tonic and served as evidence that the lads really did know what they were doing.

He calmed sufficiently for a mask to be fitted and sat with his head rested against the wall, gulping in oxygen and waiting for his other friend to be brought out.

However, minutes later, the crews confirmed the house was searched and no further casualties were located. It was good news, everyone was out.

Nobody knows how they will truly react when their life is at risk. Thought processes and reason go out the window and instinct takes over. There is no set patterns, no rules to follow. I have seen people do very strange things when their house is on fire, or when they have been involved in a road traffic collision. Injured people can spend several minutes tending to others only to collapse themselves, some wander off in a daze and completely detach from the reality of the situation, and others ask us to return to their smouldering wreck of a home to get their cigarettes.

This would not have been the first time we frantically searched a property only to find out the occupant was drinking tea at a neighbour's house. It would not have crossed their mind to let us know where they were. I relayed the information to my charge, but it did not have the reassuring effect I had expected. He insisted that there had been three of them in the house. The building was still alight, but it took a huge effort to prevent him from going back in.

The police had arrived and took over the restraining, allowing me to communicate with the BA teams. They were positive the house was empty and I trusted them implicitly.

I returned to the distressed man, now flanked by two police officers.

"There is definitely no-one else in the house. The lads know what they're doing. If anyone else was still inside, they'd have found them."

He was unrelenting: "I am telling you. There was a woman in the bedroom!"

He was pleading, saying he would go in himself, that he knew exactly where she was.

The problem was the BA crews were equally adamant

that there was no-one in the house.

The possibility of her going out the window was ruled out as the windows were sealed shut, but my watchmate Chris checked the garden as a precaution.

It was empty.

At 6ft 6 inches, Chris was the tallest on our watch. We joked that he required his own weather report. He was also the most meticulous of all of us. If it was not for Chris, the female occupant of that property would be dead.

Anyone else would have checked the garden and the bush directly underneath the bedroom window and found nothing. The shrub was as wide as it was tall. If Chris had lacked the height or the urge to have an extra look, he would never have seen the woman who had slipped between the house and the bush.

It transpired that she had fallen from the window, down the angle of the conservatory, and came to rest behind the wildly overgrown plant. A combination of alcohol, shock and freezing temperatures had caused her to pass out and she had gradually slipped out of consciousness. By the time the crews had entered the room, the heat was so intense that the windows had melted shut.

She was pulled out and brought round. Although her pulse was weak, she later made a full recovery.

Nineteen

As my work mates and I watched another sunrise together, I considered the terrifyingly tight margins by which lives can be saved or lost.

Had that first casualty remained unconscious, we may have returned to the station, oblivious to the young lady dying in her back garden.

Non-human casualties presented different problems. On one occasion, I narrowly avoided being taken out by a falling pigeon while we were attending to a fire at a pigeon coup. I looked up to find scores of unconscious pigeons raining down on us. Prize birds were flying out of the flames only to succumb to the smoke. We had the fire under control and were making progress, but the wooden structure was immaterial to the distraught owners. They argued it could be rebuilt, but it would be futile without its occupants. Our crew manager emerged as a champion to our feathered friends and single-handedly rescued dozens of pigeons thanks to some very creative use of his first aid skills.

I have also rescued my fair share of birds, but largely

from various entanglements. We were once called to liberate a bird out of a tree. Despite sounding ridiculous, the luckless creature had become snared in some netting wrapped around the tree. Unfortunately, our actions at such incidents have limited benefits. The birds are often beyond help. As much as I like animals, human casualties are always my first concern.

I understand people have a strong bond with their pets and animals in general, but some incidents suggest that maybe our priorities are a little amiss.

We were once called to a distressed bird. On arrival, we saw it was hanging upside down from a very tall building. It was caught in some mesh, marginally clinging to life.

One woman in particular was passionately rallying on the bird's behalf, insisting that we did something. She had made the call after noticing that the bird had been struggling for days.

Inadvertently, she cemented our belief that the stricken creature would not make it. Severely dehydrated, exhausted and likely to have sustained at least one broken wing, any attempt to rescue the bird would simply have been to appease the crowd. Furthermore, it was caught at least two floors above the maximum extension of our ladder.

It was a difficult decision. We could justify a request for a specialist appliance for a savable life, but not for the body retrieval of a bird.

The public, however, were oblivious to the imminent loss of life and were baying for a response.

Fortunately, we were saved by a commotion behind us.

We had our backs to the river and instinctively scanned the water, but we quickly realised that someone had collapsed on an old, disused, wooden jetty and a handful of people were desperately trying to get our attention. We instinctively legged it towards the casualty, grabbing our medical pack from the appliance on the way. It was a substantial sprint in full fire kit on a hot day, and we were panting hard by the time we arrived to find a woman unconscious on the floor. She was breathing so we placed her in the recovery position and requested an ambulance. In truth we did very little, but there was a tangible sense of relief among the onlookers. Our presence had alleviated them from both the pressure and responsibility to do something. We stayed with the casualty until the paramedics arrived and then returned to our original concern.

By the time we came back, the bird had clearly died. There was nothing we could do.

"This would never have happened if you had not all gone and ran over there!"

The woman was incandescent. "I called you. You were here to help that bird. You could have saved him, but you didn't."

At first, I thought she was joking. The whole event had played out right in front of her. She knew exactly what had happened, but she was deadly serious.

I was furious and simultaneously grateful to be laden with the medical pack. I used it as an excuse to return it to the appliance and distance myself from the scene. The vociferous bird lover was the only witness to voice her discontent, but several of the other onlookers also made their feelings clear as they closed ranks with their adopted leader and greeted us with exaggerated shakes of the head.

We had chosen human life over that of a dying pigeon and were treated as pariahs.

It was a useful lesson and a timely reminder that some people would always find fault. I realised that trying to please everyone was a futile waste of time so I began to prioritise my own needs.

I loved my work. It was fulfilling, rewarding and everything I wanted in a job. It also allowed me the time off to travel, explore and engage in activities that excited and enriched me. I treasured opportunities to challenge myself. I discovered more about myself when I was uncomfortable, cold, tired and wet, and these were the times I felt alive. I continued to captain my football team and loved playing my favourite sport with people who quickly became close friends, sharing the triumphs and the tribulations, the laughs and the losses. However, my teammates did not share my enthusiasm for white water rafting, scuba diving, triathlons, marathons and adventure races. It didn't bother me, I enjoyed the freedom of responsibility and went alone when necessary. I loved the exhilaration and the feeling of accomplishment as I savoured the post event shower and beers. It was reminiscent of pulling people from fires, but it was short lived. The feeling would pass and I would find myself craving more.

All that changed on 25th September 2005. I was out drinking with friends, celebrating my 29th birthday, when I received a phone call from my Dad. My sister had given birth to a baby boy. I had a nephew, Samuel. I made the 90-minute drive to Harrogate hospital the next day and from the second I held him in my arms, I loved him. I spent every day off with Sam, appreciating every minute. My family and I are close, but as adults we only kept in touch via phone and text messages, meeting up a few times a year. Sam was different. I was captivated by this tiny bundle of joy and possibility. I wanted to witness every milestone and enjoy every aspect of his journey. It quickly occurred to me that in my yearning for excitement and exploration, I was missing out on the greatest adventure of all time—that of parenthood.

Twenty

The birth of my nephew Samuel ignited a sense of urgency. My life was blissfully chaotic and there was still so much that I wanted to do, see and achieve, but the thought of motherhood made me consciously aware of the timescale. Obtaining a promotion was first on my to-do list.

However, my personal ambitions were irrelevant in the tumultuous final months of 2005. As the world news was dominated by the devastating aftermath of Hurricane Katrina, I said goodbye to my spiritual home.

We were merging with our neighbouring station that covered the city centre, and moving into our new purpose-built premises.

I loved my first fire station, which burst with character and industry. It was filled with fantastic personalities and good humour, but due to cuts, it was earmarked for closure.

The transfer fell on our day shift, so under the watchful eye of Nathan, we loaded and unloaded. It was sad to leave a building that held memories for so many people. The place was littered with traces of history and we salvaged some obsolete equipment and various other items for nostalgia. However, they were never adequately rehomed in the sterile, contemporary environment of the new station.

I did not want to leave the station that had come to feel like home. I enjoyed the fact that our watch spent every moment together, and the laughs shared in the open dormitory far outweighed the nuisance of the odd snorer. We had visited the new building site at various stages of the development and watched in dismay as the station took shape. We would each have our own room, but to me the privacy was akin to isolation.

"We won't see anyone," I grumbled, "everyone is going to slope off to their own room."

Paul was quick to offer a solution: "Don't worry, Kate. We can all drag our mattresses into the lecture room!"

We had two fire engines, as did the city centre. In addition, they also housed a specialist appliance, the Emergency Tender or ET. The new station had provisions for two fire engines and the ET. Four into two did not go and watches were decimated as people were transferred to neighbouring stations. James and many of the older hands decided to use the move as a catalyst for promotion. Firefighters were often reluctant to uproot themselves and leave the familiarity of a watch, but the enforced relocation created a natural opportunity to advance their career.

It was not just the station that had changed. We were now covering the majority of the city centre and that brought a disheartening amount of automatic false alarms.

We were accustomed to very busy nights of fires, road traffic accidents and other incidents. Adrenalin compensates for lack of sleep and a satisfying exhaustion is easily remedied, but getting turned out every twenty minutes to reset an alarm is exasperating, needless and tiresome.

The move took place four days before Christmas. New watches were forged overnight. We were working with different people, on new equipment, in an area that was alien to some of us, and just as we assumed all the changes were behind us, Nathan was given a permanent Watch Manager post on the White Watch at Sunderland. He had been with us for a year.

It had been an eventful 12 months. Nathan's reign had taken us through the upheaval of Adam's departure and my early months as a driver. Finally, he had taken charge through the mayhem of the move. I had assumed he would be offered the role on a permanent basis, but there was a new sheriff in town.

Simon was small in stature and loud in nature. Song lyrics would boom through the corridors and his shouts would reach you long before his little legs could. On first impression, he was a fitness enthusiast, amiable and good humoured, fastidious about buttons and standards of dress, but with a genuine interest in people. Things were looking good.

Within two months of the relocation, two lads, Harry and Mark, transferred in from other brigades around the country. They each had more time in the job, but I was now the longest serving member of the Red Watch. Despite all the upheaval, I felt a secure sense of belonging. I was content and comfortable. However, if I was going to combine a career in the fire service with motherhood, I needed to start climbing the promotion ladder.

Shortly after Simon's arrival, I made my intentions known.

"Excellent… Absolutely!" was Simon's enthusiastic response. "We will get that sorted."

Harry, Mark and Paul had also registered their interest in advancement and a training session was organised for all four of us. During it, we were to act as a crew manager and take charge of a scenario detailed by Simon. I was to be last.

The three lads were all given identical 'jobs'—a house fire, persons reported. It was bread and butter to any fire-fighter and predictably they all brought their respective incidents to a satisfactory conclusion.

Then it was my turn.

I had the benefit of hindsight and privately planned my execution of the exercise to ensure I surpassed the other candidates. I almost missed Simon's detail of my given scenario: 'OK, Kate. The drill is… an electricity pylon that has fallen onto a train carriage and burst into flames.'

There was more, but I had stopped listening. I assumed it was a joke.

"Get to work," was his order.

I did not move, my eyes followed the bark so I was able to read Simon's expression. His head slightly forward and his eyebrows raised, it was painted as questioning, but was actually confrontational. He wanted a reaction. I resolved not to give him one and turned to give a direction to my nominated driver.

Simon stopped me: "You can't use him. He has broken his leg."

Despite his newly discovered fake injury, my driver made every attempt to assist until his condition deteriorated to the extent that he was unconscious and strapped to a stretcher.

It was clearly an incident that demanded additional resources so I requested more appliances.

"You can't do that. The main scheme radio is down."

It was a ridiculous and improbable situation, patently devised for me to fail, and it was wrapped up shortly after a van full of escaped prisoners arrived on scene.

Simon concluded that it was a clear sign that I was not ready. He would rebuke my arguments with a blanket answer: "It could happen. You have to be able to show me you can cope with any scenario."

Over the coming months, I broached promotion several times, but the drills became increasingly nonsensical and I never stood a chance of managing them. It was a very public declaration that my watch manager had no faith in me. It was brutally humiliating and it hurt.

The lads were caught in the crossfire and reluctant to take sides. They were sympathetic, but supporting me came with a risk of getting thrown into my boat and many of them had yet to pass their probation. Encouragement was privately administered, but plentiful and genuine, serving as a reminder that the problem did not lie with me.

Paul had moved on, having earned a promotion, and his absence was keenly felt. However, his replacement Kian, was of a similar ilk and I loved his straight-talking approach.

The lads communicated their support through slow shakes of the head, furtive glances in Simon's direction and surreptitious 'V' signs.

With Simon in his room practising Spanish, the 22:00 film provided a safe haven for free speech.

"He's a fucking knob." Kian's succinct review of his boss went unchallenged.

Russ offered an explanation: "It's small man syndrome. He tries to make himself look bigger by putting everyone else down."

He had a point. The others had all been subjected to Simon's unique form of feedback: 'fat puff', 'streak of piss' and his old favourite, 'you should have been a lass', were regularly thrown the lads' way. Maybe I was reading too much into it.

Having positioned himself as an authority on all matters work related or otherwise, there was no sense in arguing with Simon. Despite the fact that it was never asked for, his opinion was freely given. Relationships, parenting, medical matters and private lives were all topics he considered himself an expert in. However, it soon emerged that his specialist subject was female firefighters, and more specifically that they should not be in the job. He had no cohesive argument and seemingly no basis for his opinion, just a steadfast conviction that he was right.

Simon would resolutely refrain from verbalising his thoughts in my presence. However, he was arrogant and his comments would reach me either via my work mates or when he mistakenly believed I was out of earshot.

I confronted him on several occasions, but he categorically denied there was an issue.

One particular incident, six months after Simon's arrival, suggested otherwise.

We were called to a fire at a Netto convenience store around the time they were changing hands to Asda. Because of it, their industrial bins outside were loaded with combustibles. Both bins were engulfed in flames when we arrived. I was driving, so I helped run out hose, set up the hydrant and ensured a continuous, decent supply of water.

The fire was easy enough to contain, but the shop was now smoke logged.

"Kate, put a BA set on, you and Kian are going in." Simon's order was unusual, drivers rarely wore at incidents, but I welcomed it. No-one turns down the opportunity of wearing at a job. Entering burning and smoke-filled buildings is the reason many of us joined the Fire Service, it's the role that everyone wants. Kian and I went inside, checking for any signs of fire and opening vents to clear the smoke. The shop was of considerable size, but we had completed our task well within the confines of our air supply.

We were changing our cylinders when Simon came over, and asked me to get a nearby billboard down.

I looked across to find a giant billboard. The waste units had been positioned directly below it and the flames had caught the bottom corner. It was smouldering.

My eyes creased in confusion. Kian and I were on our knees, uncomfortably sodden with exertion. There were four firefighters standing by, eager to help. It didn't make sense why he would ask me to complete the task.

Why wait for me to finish servicing my set to begin work on the billboard? Why was I the one that had to get it down?

I caught Kian's eye.

"What the..." he mouthed, equally bewildered.

I shrugged. I had no idea what was going on. My chest tightened as my shoulders felt a burden that extended far beyond the task. My mouth went dry with anticipation. There was a sinister undertone to Simon's order.

Cylinders changed, Kian and I placed our breathing apparatus sets back on the appliance. It provided a momentary sanctuary away from Simon and I took the opportunity to compose myself.

I was annoyed beyond words. I had already served a brutal four-year probation under Adam and proved myself hundreds of times under intense scrutiny from Nathan. Yet here I was, in my seventh year, undergoing a third probationary period. In contrast, the majority of my fellow firefighters had barely started their first. I could not understand why Simon had chosen to single me out.

Fine, I resolved. I would show him. I emerged from the appliance with a smile on my face. Kian followed suit.

"Oi Lurch, give us a hand with this ladder!" The 10.5 metre ladder needed a minimum of three people to lift, and Kian recruited Chris who was closest.

Chris lumbered over.

"No." Simon's outstretched arm caught Chris on the chest. "Kate can do it."

"I am doing it," I kept my voice deliberately steady and held Simon's stare. "We need one more."

"Use the short extension ladder then."

It was 3 o'clock in the morning and the temperature was below freezing, but I was burning with fury. Tears pricked, born from anger and frustration. The warm liquid stung my eyes in the night air. I blinked hard.

Solitary working went against all I had learned and everything the fire service stood for. You jumped in if someone needed a hand.

My mates were staring, hopelessly stuck in no-man's land. Wanting to help, but disinclined to go against their superior officer.

"No problem. Good idea!" I turned my back, wiping my face discreetly as I reached up for the extension ladder. It was soul crushing. Carrying the ladder through a tunnel of firefighters felt like a walk of shame, a punishment for some unknown crime. The atmosphere was horrendous. No-one knew what to say.

The lads made several attempts to get involved.

Chris tried reason: "Someone's going to need to hold the other side."

"Leave it!" Simon ordered.

"I'm going to need a drill and a torch," I shouted down to Kian.

"I hear you, Kate-o!"

I smiled. Nathan had begun the trend of linking an 'o' to everyone's name. The 'in' joke was a subtle show of solidarity.

Simon cut in, "She can get it!"

I climbed back down the ladder and walked past half a dozen firefighters on my way back to the appliance. Catching their eye, I smiled and raised my eyebrows in a determined show of nonchalance.

The task itself was unremarkable, but the height and weight of the billboard combined to make things awkward. I didn't enjoy the limelight nor the sickening thought that my manager wanted me to fail, but I took some pleasure in the united support from the lads when the billboard crashed down.

I didn't know Simon's intentions. However, if he had set out to alienate me from the watch, it misfired. There were other, less crude ways to judge someone's capabilities and I noted that over the coming months and years, no-one else was subjected to the same treatment.

As firefighters, our training is constantly assessed. Every year we attend the brigade training centre to ensure our competencies remain up to scratch. I have passed every written and practical test. But Simon was obsessively determined to find fault. Like a dog in a game of tug of war, Simon would not let up. It was not a fair fight.

Personal fulfilment masked my need for professional development. I had a fantastic social life with both my workmates and friends from football. Furthermore, I got to see my nephew Sam every week and spend some quality time with my family. I was enjoying my role as a fun auntie and I was riding a wave of happiness. While I was not pushing for promotion, Simon became a mere irritant. I thought we had reached a mutual level of tolerance if nothing else, but I was wrong.

We had been at our new station for two years and my watch and I were gathered around a TV. It had gone 23:00 hours and thoughts were beginning to turn to our beds when Simon summoned me to his office.

I was directed to sit, making the occasion slightly less formal.

Simon began: "The thing is, Kate, you haven't been yourself this past month and you don't look interested in anything."

I was stunned and had no idea where this criticism had come from. I tried to narrow it down: "When you say the past month, you don't mean last week because I was off?"

He was magnanimous enough to concede: "No, not last week."

"Or the two weeks before then when you were off?"

"No, not then."

I was livid. It was painfully apparent to me that Simon had no compelling grounds for complaint, but I desperately tried to remain composed. "So, when you say the past month, what do you mean exactly?"

"Well, this week then."

He had conceded three weeks of ground and still lacked a convincing argument.

I persisted: "I was with you on a training exercise for almost the full two days. You said everyone had done brilliantly, so you don't mean then?"

"No, not then."

We had started at ridiculous and were now entering ludicrous. Simon's discomfort was tangible. As control passed to me, I calmed down, even if I remained completely perplexed as to what was going through his head.

I continued to narrow down the time frame: "Do you mean between 3 and 5 on the second dayshift?"

He made a final desperate attempt to claim some ground: "And last night!"

I smiled inwardly, but maintained a completely neutral expression. I stayed silent for a few seconds and allowed him to enjoy his moment as I locked my eyes on his, saying:

"I was detached last night."

Detachments are used to cover short falls in staffing.

Our station had an extra firefighter, so I had taken my turn to make up the numbers elsewhere. Simon's argument was buried, but rather than give up, he tried another avenue:

"We had to do a Breathing Apparatus drill tonight because you were nearly out of date. I don't want to stop your sports leave, but I will if it's affecting your training."

Leave, detachments, sickness and other training commitments can mean that drills are hastily arranged to ensure training is kept up to date. It happens. My case was not isolated. Simon knew that, so I concluded that it was my sports leave he had a problem with. I had represented the UK Fire Brigade football team on several occasions, but he had clearly not done his research. I played ignorant. "It is a bimonthly wear, right?"

Our procedure stated that we needed to wear a breathing apparatus set at least once every two months.

"Yes, and you were nearly out of date."

"I understand that, but as my last day of sports leave was 17 months ago, I cannot see the connection."

Simon's smug, lopsided smile vanished. He was flapping now.

"You don't answer the phone!"

I almost fell off my chair. "What?"

That last swipe had caught me off guard. Simon edged forwards, sensing he was finally getting somewhere and continued: "Well, you passed it to Peter that time."

That time. It was approaching midnight and here I was

sitting in my watch manager's office to discuss a time when I did not answer the phone.

The occasion he alluded to was actually a joke. I had been sitting closest to the phone when it rang. The majority of the time, the caller is seeking an officer so Peter, our crew manager, went to reach for it. I told Peter I would get it for him and passed him the phone. It was not an incident. I recapped:

"So, when you said that I had not been myself this past month, you mean I did not answer the phone that one time, when I clearly passed it to Peter as a joke. Is that why we are here?"

"Well…" Simon was flailing, stuttering, desperate to find fault. "I have never seen you make a cup of tea."

It was a lie and it was laughable.

"Are you being serious?"

Apparently, he was. I was summoned to the office to sit through a catalogue of misrepresentations and in his fervour to admonish me, I was told in no uncertain terms to make more tea.

Twenty-One

I was conflicted—I loved my watch, but Simon's oppressive attitude was draining. The pressure to be physically capable and competent was intensified by his constant appraisal of my psyche. His stance on female firefighters was clear and I had little doubt that he wanted me off the watch. However, I sensed that he felt threatened. It was as if women firefighters compromised a masculine superiority that was entwined in his role. To admit that females were capable maybe somehow lessened his importance and standing. I drew strength from this belief and enjoyed the fact that my presence was causing my tormentor some discomfort. Besides, I'd been through so much already, I wasn't going to be bullied into a transfer. I resolved to pass every test, official or otherwise, and I dug in for a further six months.

Despite tea-gate cementing my suspicion that there was an underlying issue, I had very few options. Simon was popular amongst senior managers, a transfer would likely reflect badly on me and I'd be another lass who couldn't hack the job. I didn't have the luxury of a convenient excuse—a difficult commute, family reasons or to gain greater experience. I was single, cycled in daily and served at one of the busiest stations. I didn't want to be forced off my watch and then spend the rest of my career suffering the consequences. So, I began to search for jobs further afield. I considered buying a surf bar in Fuerteventura as it became like a second home, but the increase in All Inclusives were affecting trade. I looked at Firefighting jobs in Antarctica but couldn't get the necessary US visa, and a last minute job application for CERN was flawed when I failed to take allowances of the time difference and missed the deadline by seconds. I wasn't scared of change, but it had to be for an exciting adventure. The fact there were possibilities beyond my current situation kept me sane.

Simon's insistence that I made more tea was largely irrelevant. Our new station demographic and work routine meant tea breaks were minimal. Alongside automatic alarms, covering the city centre resulted in an upturn of lift rescues and high-rise incidents. Even water turned against us as nature caused a surge of flooding episodes. The Emergency Tender carried specialist equipment, largely for road traffic incidents involving heavy goods vehicles. It saw us attend multitudes of such incidents across the brigade area.

In a fire, we don't see anything. We use touch to get a sense of our environment and any images are formed in our mind. In a road traffic collision, the scene is laid out before us—a visual carnage.

Nobody really knows how they will react when they

are presented with casualties who sustain horrific injuries. I remember having an overwhelming fear that my first encounter would result in me freezing or throwing up.

It actually came during my second set. We were in another station's area, returning from a house fire, and control directed us via the radio. I vividly recall three elements of detail: "Car overturned. Multiple casualties. Motorcyclist involved."

It was my first road traffic incident and it sounded horrific. I had less than three minutes to prepare myself. I pulled my high visibility jacket over my fire kit, fixed my goggles and imagined the absolute worst-case scenario. Then I convinced myself I could deal with it.

The actual scene was stretched over the carriageway and was not pretty. We were the first emergency service on site so I was dropped off with a first aid pack to deal with the stricken motorcyclist while the others continued on to the car. That experience has possibly helped me comprehend my role at future road traffic incidents. One casualty at a time, focus entirely on them and everything else is irrelevant. Fortunately, at that particular incident, the motorcyclist was taken by air ambulance and was expected to make a full recovery.

The wellbeing of the casualties is at the forefront of any rescue. In the event of multiple casualties, we divide our resources accordingly. If a paramedic is in attendance, we'll take the lead from them, as they are able to determine which casualties require more urgent attention. We're not there to apportion blame and everyone is treated on an equal basis.

I've not become immune to haunting images, but they're stored away in a section of my mind that I only open if I choose to. It's not something I would share with friends or family. However, we do talk it through on a watch level, on the way back to the station, maybe over the mess table or even over a beer. It's customary for firefighters to engage in black humour over such incidents. It's not disrespectful, but rather a necessary coping mechanism sometimes. Life has to go on.

We wear a uniform for a variety of reasons. For me, being able to take it off at the end of the shift is as important as any.

Post-traumatic stress is prevalent in the service and no-one is immune. The accumulative cost of the physical demands of firefighting is well-documented. However, the brain's ability to process increasing amounts of harrowing scenes is largely unknown. It cannot be fixed with a period of rest, nor can it be permanently erased. The horrible, stomach turning feeling surrounding the sudden loss of life, and the haunting screams of recently bereaved families will forever be etched in my memory.

Incidents affected my workmates in different ways. Some found fatalities in people of their age particularly difficult to comprehend. While others were traumatised by the death of a dog. Simon, however, appeared completely devoid of sentiment and empathy, and encouraged others to follow suit. His rabid need to find fault and weakness in individuals ensured that feelings and emotions were off limits in his company.

My resilience was my downfall. I was so consumed by the need to prove myself, I was blinded to the fact that it was futile. My actions made no lasting impact on Simon's views, I was merely treading water.

My life had become a whirlpool. It was a frenzy of activity, but the birth of my second nephew ultimately made me realise I was not getting anywhere. My brother's son, Oliver, was born in March 2008. Desperate to meet him, I made the hour journey to Northallerton as soon as I heard the news. I held him in my arms and, just as I had with Sam 30 months previously, I fell in love.

I stayed over at Dom's house, sharing in my brother's celebrations and marvelling at the new life and the exciting journey that lay ahead of him. My own hopes and aspirations catapulted to the forefront of my mind on my journey home. My first solo trip abroad had opened up a whole new world to me and I had ticked off several items from my bucket list. Since my introduction to surfing, I began snowboarding, took a road trip around the west coast of Canada, completed the Edinburgh marathon and the London Triathlon, and started up my own Women's Football Team—Whickham Fellside, with whom I competed in the Durham County Football League.

Each achievement cemented a belief that I could achieve anything I wanted. The problem was that my deepest desires contradicted each other. I valued my independence and did not want a partner, but I longed for a family. I started imagining children every time I went for a walk. Always two, sometimes a boy and a girl, sometimes two boys. They would run along and play happily and I would smile—with hope rather than expectation.

I was desperate for a new challenge and aspired to progress in my career, but I needed to do it on my terms and to prove Simon wrong. Something had to give.

Twenty-Two

It was Chris who first planted the seed of adoption in my mind. I knew that he and his wife had been through the adoption process in the hope of a younger sister for their son, Rory, but my interest was really piqued when their gorgeous little girl came home.

Chris was dependable. A giant of a man who never seemed in a rush, he told things as they were, without embellishments or fanfare. He stuck to the facts. I took this incredible opportunity to obtain as much information as I could.

"Can anyone adopt?"

"Pretty much. But you need to remember that these kids may have had a really bad start. You need to be able to offer a loving, stable home."

"Oh, I could do that!"

Chris looked at me, his steely blue eyes fixed on mine. He asked the most basic question and all my hopes were dashed.

"Who will have the kids when you're at work?"

I clearly hadn't thought it through, but I was not about to be swayed.

"OK, so if I sort that out? Do you think they would consider me? Without a partner?"

"I guess, but you would need a really good support network around you." As if reading my thoughts, Chris added, "It's a pity your family doesn't live closer."

He was right. I considered applying for a transfer and moving back to North Yorkshire, but every solution came with further problems. House prices in Nidderdale had rocketed and I couldn't afford anywhere close to my parents. Equally, I could be posted to another part of the region, with no friends or family nearby. A day shift job in an office would solve childcare issues, but motherhood would come at the cost of my career and everything I had worked so hard for. It was a difficult decision and I was not ready to make it.

I needed something else to focus on, so I became an instructor for the Young Firefighters Association. It ran alongside my current role, but provided an opportunity for self-development and, more significantly, experience working with children.

I also set about ticking off more life goals.

In 2009, I climbed Kilimanjaro, gaining as much from my experience in the local area as I did from the summit of the mountain. I routinely use hostels when I travel. They're usually well situated and I enjoy meeting like-minded people. My first experience of Tanzania coincided with a global outbreak of swine flu and all Arusha airport staff were dressed in full body decontamination suits complete with masks, so only their eyes were visible as they silently ushered us through arrivals. It was a necessary precaution, but I found it unnerving and was grateful to get to a taxi.

I took a seat in the front and was startled when someone climbed in the back, behind the driver who smiled across at me.

"This is my friend, he works at the airport so I give him a lift home. That is ok?"

I watched as we passed endless high gates each topped with security fences until we pulled up outside one and the driver beeped his horn.

My host was a friendly soul in her mid-forties, she bustled around the hostel showing me around and introducing me to the other residents. They were each preparing a communal meal, and within minutes I was enjoying their hospitality. It transpired that many of them had lived there for several years and were involved in supporting various projects around the city. They lived simply, pooled resources and enjoyed a remarkable community spirit. It can be argued that true altruism doesn't exist as foreign volunteering programmes are sold on the countless benefits to the individual. Furthermore, while the motivation to help others is admirable, there's a danger that the culture of western saviour volunteerism, combined with our desire to sell ourselves on social media, can perpetuate stereotypes of Africa while collapsing its many nations into one. Obliviously, I also took photos of local children before realising I would never take a photograph of a stranger's child at home. The individuals I met during my short time in Arusha, both local people and those at the hostel, were passionate about establishing links, listening and learning.

I spent my afternoons at a project where the focus was on building, and I felt more at home doing something physical. I was motivated by a desire to help, but admittedly my primary focus was to feel useful. I wanted to contribute to the overall effort and earn my spot at the table. A few of us worked on a play area. It wasn't requested, or necessary, but it occupied our hands, quenched our industrious nature and helped us feel included. I loved being surrounded by children, sharing their laughs and listening to their stories. They energised me and I knew beyond all doubt that I wanted children in my life.

I returned home invigorated by a successful summit and began to steer my life in a different direction. In June 2010, I moved out of my flat and bought a three-bedroom house on the outskirts of town. I chose the area specifically with children in mind and I shared my life changing news with the lads.

"I've decided to adopt!" I declared as we separated from our morning parade.

The lads laughed. "You?! You can't adopt. When are you going to have time to walk a dog?!"

"I don't want to adopt a dog. I want to adopt children!"

The call out system sprung into life and the piercing tone reverberated around the station. However, it was the sound of laughter that rang in my ears as I climbed into the rear cab.

I couldn't blame the lads for the hysterics following my announcement—I had no partner, no family close by and I worked night shifts. I was hardly an ideal candidate for an adoptive parent, but I was determined to make it happen. For now, however, I sat in a huff, arms folded, staring out the window for the duration of the journey to the bariatric incident.

Increasingly we were being requested to help larger people. Sometimes it was just a matter of assisting someone wedged in the bath, but often it was altogether more serious and time critical.

As firefighters, we endeavour to ensure that everyone is treated with dignity and respect. We encounter casualties in a multitude of acutely embarrassing situations. Discretion and professionalism are at the heart of our response and we make every effort to curtail any discomfort, but consideration must be given to the constraints of time and on some occasions casualties have to be removed by any means necessary.

At this particular incident, the occupier had died, several days, if not weeks earlier. Unfortunately, this information did not reach us until we opened the door and my olfactory sense soared into overdrive. The faeces of three dogs littered the house and the deceased needed to be carried downstairs. The task was poignantly unpleasant. A man, not much older than me, had died alone in a flat and the only indicator of his passing was the nuisance of the barking dogs.

People do not become firefighters for the praise or the recognition. We are largely faceless, our presence a blur, almost incidental to the bigger picture. A means to an end. The overwhelming majority of our work goes unreported, carried out behind closed doors, often in the dead of night.

It is a privilege to be there when someone needs you. An opportunity to make a difference. You witness the rawest moments and share exhilarating highs. However, it also has a habit of putting things in perspective. My own concerns and difficulties were dwarfed by the huge struggles I saw others go through.

The most heartbreaking and expressive statistic was the number of suicides and attempted suicides we attended. Our presence at a notorious bridge was almost a daily occurrence. Sadly, our attendance was often superfluous and body recovery was left to the boat crew.

There were times when a suicide attempt was clearly a cry for help and we would remain in attendance at a pre-determined location, away from the immediate area and inconspicuous so as not to cause alarm. The individual concerned would receive the support and care they needed, but it would often take several hours for the professionals to coerce them to a place of safety. Our resources might be stretched, but firefighters remain at an incident as long as they are needed.

Our role is not confined to extinguishing fires and cutting people from cars. It is about doing anything possible to improve a stranger's circumstance.

It may involve searching for a casualty's severed fingers in a rat-infested underpass, long after they have been transported to hospital. Or administering oxygen to a treasured family pet. Or it might mean salvaging anything possible from a flooded home.

Episodes of flooding have increased dramatically in recent years and inevitably lead to a high volume of calls. The control room is often forced to divert callers to another area of the country where they will be told they are in a queue and help will arrive when it is available. It is not what you want to hear when your home is submerged in dirty flood water. Firefighters do not have a statutory duty to assist in incidents of flooding, but provide 24-hour assistance whenever they are needed.

I would wager that the overwhelming majority of people who have needed the fire service would testify to our worth, but frustratingly it seems there is a continuous stream of people who question every action we take.

The winter of 2010 became known as the Big Freeze. Heavy snowfalls made driving treacherous, and a six-mile slog in knee-high snow was the only way I could guarantee getting to work on time. Against all odds, my entire watch were present for the start of shift. Even Andy, our crew manager, who had covered 12 miles on foot. We had all missed breakfast and no-one had the time to collect food items on their way in. So, we made our way to the nearest grocery store for provisions. I was photographed by a taxi driver who captured me leaving the shop with bread and milk. A copy of the photograph was sent to my chief, with a demand to know why I was out shopping. Fortunately, our most senior officer was of the opinion that even firefighters had to eat.

We were on shift over Christmas, but my friend Lindsey had recently become a housemate and I had company over the festive period. The arrangement was temporary as she had sold her flat and was looking for somewhere else, but I quickly adjusted to sharing my space and enjoyed the companionship. For the first time since Sophie moved south, I had someone to offload to on a daily basis. As Lindsey became increasingly exasperated over Simon's antics, I began to see his behaviour from a neutral perspective.

Our illustrious leader had an obsession with drills. Contrary to Adam's belief, Simon's conviction was that you did drills to be good at drills. To be more accurate, one particular drill: putting the 13.5 metre ladder up to the third floor of the drill tower. We were specialists at it and every probationer assigned to our watch sailed through their much-rehearsed exams. Simon was a perfectionist and flawlessly executed ladder drills were imperative to him. The precision was manufactured and a ridiculously large amount of time was dedicated to performing that one drill.

Amateurs practice until they get it right. Professionals practice until they never get it wrong. We were professionals, but we were also human.

The last traces of a heavy snowfall were still visible on

the station yard. January had barely begun and we had a visitor. A young man who had aspirations of a career in the fire service had asked to trial some of the tests prior to his assessment day. To enable this, the 13.5 metre ladder needed to be pitched.

Four of the lads were scrambled to put the ladder in position. It wobbled slightly on the icy ground, but nestled perfectly in place.

We spent the morning running through what would be expected on each test and the candidate left at lunchtime confident and grateful. The afternoon was fairly nondescript, and none of us had a clue that the events of the morning had angered our watch manager.

It was only when we reported for duty the next evening at 1800 hours that we realised we had collectively been sent to Coventry.

Simon refused to speak to any of us. In the event that something needed to be communicated he would grunt, gesticulate excessively or attempt ventriloquism. I had drawn the short straw and was his nominated driver for the 15 hours' night shift. He did not utter a single word unless it was absolutely necessary. We attended a person threatening to jump and sat in silence for two hours. The next night was more of the same. It was laughable. Simon was in his mid-fifties, but his actions were more akin to a 5-year-old's.

Fortunately, we were accustomed to dealing with our childish officer in charge. He festered in his room for two night shifts and revealed the cause of his strop the next set:

the ladder slipping on the ice.

To the untrained eye, it was unnoticeable. To the trained eye, it was totally understandable. To Simon, it was unforgivable. Consequently, we spent the entire day putting up the ladder and taking it back down again.

Dusk signed off a day of faultless drills and Simon announced we had been pardoned. However, the whole ludicrous episode had come at a price: the last remnants of respect I had for the man in charge.

I believe that things happen for a reason, and on reflection I can see that as my desire to be a mother grew, my tolerance for Simon's behaviour dwindled.

We were busy. The demanding schedule of incidents and false alarms meant we spent more time getting dressed than sleeping on a night shift. We had become accustomed to the seemingly incessant tone of the call out system and the sickly, lightheaded tiredness that accompanied our journey home. Red eyed detachments wandered aimlessly around the station for the final hour of the night shift, vowing never to return, but we loved it.

I did not want to be anywhere else. However, Simon became unbearable.

Chris and I were wearing at a high-rise job, laden with breathing apparatus sets, hose, first aid and breaking in equipment. The fire was easily extinguished, however an open riser outlet on a lower floor had caused a flood. The site manager provided a mop and bucket, but first all our gear needed to be returned to the appliance. I volunteered to take it back.

I always opted to do the job that requires the most effort, it was intrinsic, but it also kept Simon off my back. Chris argued, but relented, fully aware of the situation.

I was placing the breathing apparatus sets onto the back of the appliance, when the driver's radio crackled. It was Simon:

"If anyone has eyes on that lazy cow, can you send her upstairs to help Chris with the mopping!"

Russ spun round from behind the wheel. "What is his problem?!"

"Tell him I'm on my way."

I marched up the twelve flights of stairs, red faced with exertion and anger, and arrived to find Chris leaning on the mop, chatting to the site manager and Peter, our crew manager, who looked surprised to see me.

"What are you doing here?"

"Apparently I need to give Chris a hand?"

"It only took two minutes, Kate. We're coming back down now."

I was fuming and stormed into Simon's office back at the station.

His eyes widened, but he could barely stifle a grin as he explained the radio message away as a misunderstanding. My patience was diminishing. I knew then that my time on the red watch was coming to an end.

A week later, Kian was reprimanded after he returned my lottery tin to the secure cupboard following the weekly collection. It was absurd, we are almost programmed to operate as a team and help each other out, but I was accustomed to being the exception. No-one was allowed to do anything for me.

Kian was dumbfounded as he offered some mitigation: "But Kate took the shop tin out of the cupboard for me?!"

This was my manager's response:

"It's nothing personal, but I need to make sure people are not doing things for Kate, because she could end up like Bridget."

It was an excessive reaction to one individual. Bridget had left six years earlier, most of our current watch had never even worked with her, but she had become the mean setting for female firefighters. It was exasperating. My situation would never improve while my watch manager insisted on comparing me to a firefighter in the distant past simply because of my gender. I never once heard a male colleague compared to another, but my predicament was not helped by Simon's superiors.

They closed ranks and refused to acknowledge a problem. When I explained that my line manager would not speak to me, a senior member of staff laughed, 'Well, we all know what he's like.'

I confided in another and detailed a series of occasions when I had been unfairly targeted. They also expressed amusement. As hilarious as senior management found my situation, it had become untenable to me.

I was the senior hand on the watch, having been there

longer than any of my colleagues, yet I was forced to submit a transfer request.

I handed Simon the form along with an explanation: "I'm leaving. I cannot work with you."

His reaction was typical of our working relationship.

'Smashing, that's great.'

It spoke volumes that after seven years working together, I was afforded three words.

I decided to request a move to West Denton as it would be nearer to my home. I knew Dave, the manager of the red watch, and I had heard good things about Ray, the man in charge of the white watch. I wanted to make sure that my new manager would be happy to have me on his team, so I spoke to Dave and then rang Ray from my car, explaining that if I moved, I needed to be on a watch where I would feel welcome.

Ray's response restored my belief in the fire service.

"Of course Kate, we would love to have you."

It was an amazing feeling. Immediately I felt lighter and full of hope. Dave and Ray were genuine guys and would be brilliant bosses. I had no doubt that I would really enjoy working for either of them. However, until someone was prepared to take my place on the least desirable shift in the brigade, thanks to Simon's notoriety, I could not transfer to another operational post.

My position on the watch had become unsustainable, but I was stuck.

A constant stream of recruits had sanctioned the secure

passage of previous deserters from the watch, but there had been a recruitment freeze. I had missed the last safety vessel and was trapped indefinitely.

There was one last hope, a haven in the form of community fire safety.

It was not a department people chose to work for. The physical aspect of firefighting, the comradeship and the intensity of life and death situations are intoxicating. The office could not compete and consequently there was often a shortage of firefighters in the department.

The timing was ideal, as they were looking for someone to commit for three months and I wanted an exit strategy. In fairness to Simon, he didn't stand in my way and for the first time in my life I was working from 9 till 5.

I didn't want to leave my watch, nor the friends I considered as brothers. It was a gut-wrenching loss and the first few weeks felt like a grieving process. At first I was in shock, everything happened so quickly, it took a while to process. Then I was angry. I felt I had been forced off the only watch I had known. Sadness followed, as I felt the loss more acutely, all the happy memories flooded back and I seriously contemplated rescinding my transfer request. However, I came to realise it was my pride that had suffered most. I had built up a reputation and was respected across the red watch as a capable firefighter. I would be leaving all that behind and starting again.

Finally came acceptance. I realised there was no going back. Everything had changed. I needed to move forward, deal with the past and take ownership of my decision.

I went into Simon's office for the last time.

"I want to apologise. I should not have said that I am leaving because of you. I'm not. I'm leaving because of me, I have stayed on the same watch for too long and I need to move on."

Simon nodded, his eyes fixed on mine.

"In fact," I continued. "I wanted to thank you. I've had a fantastic time on the red watch and a lot of that is down to you. So, thank you!"

I extended a hand and he took it. I was now free to move forward.

Like the majority of firefighters in the Prevention and Education department, I didn't plan on being there. It was a means to an end. The majority of my new colleagues were injured. One was reassigned after suffering memory loss following meningitis. Determined to see out his final two years of service on the trucks, he requested a second opinion, but when he forgot to attend his appointment, he had to concede the medical professionals may have a point.

I had mistakenly believed that the Prevention and Education department conducted home safety checks all day and every day. I could see the value of fitting smoke alarms and discussing escape plans in people's homes, but they were not the reason I became a firefighter. The three-month secondment would afford me distance from Simon and some thinking time. I had not anticipated that it would give me so much more.

Twenty-Three

I had been a firefighter for 12 years and served my entire career on the same watch. My heart would be irrevocably attached to the brothers I worked with and the good times we shared. I was reluctant to say goodbye and took every opportunity to meet the lads for a drink.

The pubs in Ouseburn were a favoured route and when we reached the Free Trade Inn, Russ and I sat in the beer garden reminiscing. Our joint history was bursting with happiness and good times. The evocative memories induced giggles, guffaws and tears to my eyes. After a while however, the tales subsided and the merriment was replaced with a comfortable silence. I looked out onto the river.

"Where did it all go wrong, Russ?" I mused. "We had such a laugh."

My mate responded with incredible emotive integrity. "The thing is, you do what is right. I do what is easy."

I turned towards him and was shocked to see a lost, desolate expression etched on his face. I suddenly realised that I was not the only one struggling. Our watch had been a stronghold, a constant in both our lives, and it was crumbling. The personalities on our watch were not predisposed to conflict and were reluctant to challenge Simon. They may have taken the path of least resistance, but looking up at my oldest firefighter friend, I do not believe anyone had it easy.

Simon was a difficult, complex character and a great deal of time and energy was invested into managing his moods. The majority of the watch were still in their probation and did not want to risk upsetting their officer in charge. This was compounded by the fact they were all decent human beings who simply wanted to please. I had spent my entire career assuaging my line managers. I couldn't blame the lads for doing the same.

It had taken me a considerable amount of time to realise that my worth was not measured by the opinions of others, nor was it my responsibility to justify my appointment. My journey had been filled with exasperation, self-doubt and disappointment. I wanted better for my friends, but we each had to find our own way.

Over the coming months, Chris and Kian also transferred watches. We were all working on different shift patterns, with new workmates and attending separate incidents. It was perhaps inevitable that we drifted apart.

I cannot regret the time I spent on the red watch. I loved the lads, the variety of incidents and the volume of calls. I also enjoyed the comfortable feeling of familiarity around the station, but it was irrefutably the right time to move on.

Prevention and Education was largely lone working,

but as a newcomer, alien to my responsibilities, I needed a mentor. At six feet tall, Ben was a stereotypical burly fire-fighter with 27 year's operational experience. The repercussions of viral meningitis had forced him into the office, but provided Ben with a fresh outlook on life and priorities. He entered his 50th year with vivacity and enthusiasm for his new role. I could not have wished for a better partner.

Firefighters are in the business of saving lives, and preventing fires has a huge role to play. Fitting smoke alarms in domestic properties and educating people on fire safety had led to a significant decrease in house fires and fatalities. Consequently, Home Safety Checks have been an integral part of every firefighter's workload since the aftermath of the 2002 strike. However, the specialist nature of the department meant that we visited the most vulnerable groups, the higher risk households and the more colourful characters.

On one particular morning, Ben and I called at an address to complete a Home Safety Check. It was an upstairs flat and the pungent smell of cigarettes hit me as soon as the door was opened. Ascending the stairs, we emerged into a smoke cloud. It was an atmosphere that made you appreciate fresh air. Ben set about fitting smoke alarms as I directed my talk to the elderly lady of the house. Her son surfaced from his room, roll-up in hand to join in the conversation.

Ben merged with us on the landing as I finished my questions.

"Does anyone smoke in bed?"

The mother was taken aback, clearly shocked and

affronted, she responded with some considerable force.

"Nobody smokes in this house!"

It was my turn to be stunned. My eyes involuntarily narrowed as I gawped at her in confusion. A quick glance at Ben confirmed I was not going mad, before we both turned and stared at the son.

With one arm now strategically placed behind a door, he appeared a vision of innocence as he reinforced his mother's words.

"That's right." He was shaking his head, silently pleading with Ben and I. "Nobody smokes in this house."

The dear old lady proudly announced,

"He knows I would not stand for it!"

We left her in blissful ignorance, but well protected by numerous smoke alarms.

On another occasion, we were called to fix a faulty alarm. The warning devices we fit have a 10-year lifespan. The low battery indicator is an intermittent beep, designed to be extremely irritating so action is taken. We stood underneath the offending detector and listened for confirmation. Seconds turned into minutes as Ben, myself and the resident, all stared at an alarm that had not made a single noise.

I cracked first.

"I can't hear anything."

Ben concurred,

"That's not making any noise."

"Exactly!"

The man was animated.

"It hasn't made a single noise since you fitted it!"

It took us several minutes to convince him that it would only activate in a fire situation.

Acting with extreme professionalism, we ensured we were safely out of earshot before collapsing in hysterics.

"You'll miss all this when you go back on the trucks."

Ben was right.

I was really appreciating my time in the department. I loved having responsibility for my own workload, a supportive manager and a partner like Ben, but my heart lay on the operational side. I was 35 years old and wanted to go to incidents for as long as my fitness and health allowed.

"Maybe you don't need to go back on the trucks to be happy. This job would be much easier when the children come along!"

I turned to the man who had become a good friend. He had been extremely supportive of my adoption idea and made a compelling, but futile argument. I wanted to be a mum and a firefighter. I wasn't looking for a compromise and I didn't want to give up on my dream job just because it would be easier.

As it happened, my three-month secondment extended into a year before my transfer finally came through for the white watch at West Denton. It had been a frustrating twelve months. I was desperate to get back to riding fire engines and was annoyed that my career had effectively been placed on hold. However, the department had given me a different perspective.

Lifting the Fire Hydrant Lid

I found the role rewarding and empowering. I had spent a dozen years operating inside the bubble and protective shield of a watch. A strong team unit can be unbeatable. However, it can also create an atmosphere of compliance. I feel I needed those twelve months to find myself again.

Twenty-Four

I completed the necessary refresher training and loved being back at the thick end of the action—putting out fires and cutting people out of cars. My new watch manager, Ray, was immediately accepting and wonderfully supportive. He treated his team as adults and their adherence was born from love and respect. It was an alien sensation. Ray did not look for problems and I was no longer the senior hand—there were firefighters with almost thirty years' service. I loved listening to their stories and learning from their experience. Most of the younger lads had around ten years in the job. They were all fitness enthusiasts with confident and upbeat personalities. The amalgamation of characters throughout the watch created a buoyant aura—a far cry from the constant put downs on Simon's watch. It took a few sets for me to relax, to realise that the past was behind me. I didn't realise that I had been carrying negative baggage until I began to feel lighter.

I thrived in the atmosphere of mutual respect and thoroughly enjoyed my time at work. I had spent so many years seeking acceptance and tirelessly proving myself in an environment that was hostile to my efforts, to be instantly recognised as an equal felt like a rare gift and I treasured it. I could see with a depressing clarity that it had taken me over a decade to achieve something my male counterparts had taken for granted from their very first day. I cannot speak highly enough of the firefighters and management team of my new watch. It was a brilliant mix of youth and experience, professionalism and humour. A group of people who were confident in their abilities, both as individuals and as a unit, every single person came to work with a smile on their face. This was my firefighting utopia.

I was settled, happy and comfortable. My football team were flying high in the league and formed the basis of some brilliant friendships as we enjoyed some fantastic holidays together. We were in Orlando, Florida, when Sam's brother, George, was born in August 2012. A month later, as we celebrated Sam's 7th birthday, the river Swale burst its banks, flooding the nearby roads. However, Dom and his wife, Kate, miraculously made it to Northallerton hospital where my beautiful niece, Isabel, was also born.

My life was as perfect as it had ever been. I could not imagine a better time to start a family.

Ben put me in touch with a friend of his who had recently adopted, and her advice was invaluable.

"The adoption process can be difficult and painful. It requires you to go over everything in your life and revisit times which you may prefer to keep hidden. But you realise it's necessary and, eighteen months on, I'm sitting here with my little boy. It has absolutely been worth it."

Eighteen months to complete the adoption process was news to me. It had taken three years for Chris' little girl to be placed, but even if I was working to a tighter time scale, I reasoned I had plenty of time to get on the promotion ladder while I went through the programme.

Sitting around the table at Christmas, surrounded by my family, I was categorical.

"I am definitely ready to adopt. I'm going to make the call."

My family were overjoyed, but I had to rein them in.

"It will take at least 18 months and I still have no idea if I'll be accepted."

It was true. I was single, I worked shifts and I had no family close by. However, second guessing the adoption criteria was driving me crazy. I needed to know for sure.

On 16th January 2013, I finally made the call. I had taken the first meaningful step of a journey that was to change my life.

Twenty-Five

Two weeks later an adoption worker visited me at home. It was an informal chat, but my dream rested on the outcome. Consequently, I spent the entire day cleaning the house.

Melanie arrived at 6pm, a pleasant, voluptuous lady with a kind face and a smile that put me instantly at ease. We chatted for an hour in the lounge. I was slightly disappointed that after all my efforts she only saw one room.

Melanie explained that there were very few barriers to anyone who wanted to adopt. There were hurdles, but these could be negotiated. The fact I was single was not a huge problem as nurseries and childminders could be used while I worked. A support network was vital, but it didn't have to comprise of family members—close, understanding friends were acceptable substitutes and I was very fortunate in that department.

I contained my excitement until Melanie had left, then spent several minutes punching the air. Adoption had been my dream for several years and now it was a very real possibility. It felt amazing.

I updated my boss, Ray, the next day. He had been so supportive from the outset, I owed him the courtesy of honesty and openness.

"Does that mean you'll be leaving us?"

I laughed and explained the time scales. It had taken me 12 years to find a manager like Ray, I had no intention of leaving anytime soon.

A month after my initial meeting with Melanie, I attended an adoption information course. It involved a Tuesday and a Thursday evening, followed by a full weekend.

I arrived late on that first night. I had to negotiate rush hour in the city centre, so predicting problems, offered my apologies in advance. I was only five minutes late, but the session had started and the door was locked. I peered through the glass pane and very nearly turned back.

The seats were arranged in a horseshoe, I could see two sides fully and the backs of heads from the side nearest me. I instantly realised that everyone in the room seemed to look like parents. Warm and sensible grown-ups, complying effortlessly to a smart, yet casual, unofficial dress code. I looked down at my hoody, jeans and trainers. At 36 years old, they were still staples of my wardrobe.

My life was not exactly conventional and I had no cause to see myself as a grown up. Nobody would describe me as 'Mumsy'. In fact, I assumed they would be more likely to say, 'I cannot imagine you with kids.' Maybe I wasn't ready.

The thing with glass panes though, is it works both

ways. While I had my nose pressed against the glass, peering around the room, Melanie spotted me and opened the door. I apologised and made for the one remaining empty seat. A voice followed me,

"Don't worry, we've just started. We're going through what we expect from you on the course."

I took my seat and looked up at the screen. There in big capital letters were the words TIME KEEPING.

Despite not getting off to a great start, I really enjoyed the evening. I found myself sitting next to another single girl and a gay couple. Aside from us, there were five heterosexual couples. I had not arrived with any preconceived ideas of what the course would be like or who I would meet, and I was surprised at how liberating I found discussing adoption with other prospective adopters to be. We shared a common bond and with that came mutual support for each other.

We were bombarded with information and hand-outs. We watched DVDs, sat through PowerPoint presentations and worked in small groups. We talked a great deal about the process and the various steps we needed to take. The programme appeared impossibly long, but I was prepared for that. I was happy to take it one stage at a time, knowing I was moving ever closer to my dream of being a mum.

I was amongst the first to arrive for our second session on Thursday night. I honoured the unspoken rule that is universally observed, 'always use the same chair', and settled proudly into my seat. However, my smugness vanished when I realised that everyone else had writing materials and were intent on making notes.

Again, I questioned if I was doing the right thing. My course mates were clearly more organised and seemed altogether more engaged with the whole process. I listened to what was being said and contributed fully to discussions and group tasks, learning an enormous amount, but I got the distinct impression that they had already researched a great deal before arriving at this point.

I am in no way an extrovert, but I have a quiet confidence in myself. I was not overawed by my fellow participants, but I had to question whether I had given the whole adoption idea enough thought. The couples would have spent countless hours discussing whether this was the right option for them. They had a shoulder to lean on in times of doubt. They could voice their fears and reassure each other.

The other single girl and I did not have that, although as she lived with her parents, she would have had to persuade them as much as herself that she was ready. I only needed to convince myself. My friends and family were supportive and would periodically check in to make sure I had properly thought things through. I assured them that I had and was almost blasé about how I would cope.

My friends that had children had moved to the edge of my social radar. As parents, their priorities had changed and I did not see as much of them. Having had no experience themselves, my childless friends did not take much convincing that I could manage. In the event that I wanted positive reinforcement, I would seek out an obliging friend and phrase a question to get the response I needed. Maybe I could have taken more time, asked more questions and discussed adoption with more people, but I don't feel that would have made a difference. I had decided and that was all I needed.

The following Saturday, I packed some lunch and writing materials and left my house at 07:30 hours. I arrived confident and relaxed for the 09:00 start. That weekend we were led through a maze of scenarios which result in children being taken into care and visitors were weaved into the fabric of the course—couples who had adopted brought their precious children in and spoke of their experiences, and a birth mother courageously told of how her children had been taken into care. She was far removed from the stereotype of an alcohol and drug fuelled unfit mother, and completely changed my uneducated perception that she had made choices. She herself had been an unfortunate victim of circumstances, robbed of a childhood she dragged herself through adolescence. She had been denied the opportunity to learn life skills that I took for granted and stood no chance of being able to look after a baby. However, it was the grandad who had the greatest impact on me. My heart went out to him as he expressed, with great vulnerability, his helplessness when the grandchildren he doted on were taken into care. Seeing the wider repercussions of adoption really brought home to me the enormity of what lay ahead.

Throughout the preparatory stage of the process we

covered countless potential problems that could be encountered through a child's life. Many of us take a happy childhood for granted. I never recognised a need to consider self-preservation through the eyes of a child.

I'm acutely aware that there are very few certainties in life. There would be no magic cures or overnight miracles, but the course repeatedly demonstrated that time, love and understanding could produce remarkable results.

I had never believed that adopting children would be easy. However, as the information stage of the process concluded and the sheer volume of needs and possible pitfalls became apparent, I began to question whether I was properly equipped to care for siblings.

I couldn't imagine life without my brothers and sister; they were integral to who I was. I loved growing up in a big family and always assumed I would have more than one child. I also knew that sibling groups were harder to place. The heart wrenchingly cruel scenario of losing your parents and then being ripped away from your closest allies was unfathomable. Those were the children I desperately wanted to help.

The course was exhausting. I was mentally drained by the end of the weekend, but it meant I was now able to formally apply. Due to the enormous amount of work required to complete a Prospective Adopters Report, it was prudent to ensure the applicants were fully aware of all the aspects and potential problems before proceeding. I was as determined as ever and my home visits were underway in mid-March, just two weeks after finishing the course.

I had made a 9.30am appointment. I was coming off night shifts and due to finish at 09:00, it was only a five-minute drive to my house. The trouble was that emergencies do not conform to a set shift pattern and I left the station nearly an hour late. I rang Melanie, who immediately put me at ease, she was happy to wait. However, it was a timely reminder that previously insignificant factors, such as casual overtime, could have huge implications to my application. Arranging childcare for set times was one thing, but there were no guarantees with incidents. I pushed my concerns to one side and focused on the task at hand.

The majority of that first visit involved verifying my identification and completing a Criminal Records Bureau (CRB) form for an enhanced disclosure while Melanie checked over my home for any potential safety problems or risks.

My life was frenetic. I was juggling work and an increasingly hectic fixture schedule as the football season heated up. I would visit my family as much as possible, desperate not to miss a single milestone in the lives of my precious nephews and niece. I had also decided to undergo some major home improvements and drew up plans to update both my kitchen and bathroom. The whirlwind would calm for the duration of the subsequent home visits and my adoption application progressed quietly, but efficiently in the background.

Ironically, my two biggest concerns regarding my eligibility to adopt suddenly appeared to work in my favour. The fact I was single effectively halved the workload for Melanie, and as I was back working shifts, I was more readily available. Therefore, when my adoption course reconvened 8 weeks later, at the start of May, I was only one visit away from completion. We had covered every conceivable aspect of my life; childhood, school life, my parents and my siblings, relationships, finances, work life and my experiences with children.

I enjoyed recalling a happy childhood and revisiting my school days. I didn't find the visits particularly invasive, and I understood the need to establish if I was capable of meeting the emotional and financial needs of a child. Furthermore, it allowed Melanie to see the complete me, supported by references from several key players in my life. This, I was told, would be invaluable when it came to the matching process. Overall, I found it a very cathartic experience, revisiting my past and preparing for an exciting future.

As we said our goodbyes at the end of the weekend, my new adoption friends and I vowed to keep in touch. It was surreal to think that the next time we met we could all be parents.

On my last home visit, we completed the final and hardest part of the assessment process—the checklist.

The checklist contains a list of medical conditions, behavioural concerns, development issues and other needs of a potential child. For each one, there are three options—'yes', 'no' and 'will discuss'. I found it extremely difficult and acutely humbling to discover that I was not as decent as I thought. Perhaps in parts, I could hide behind the fact I was single. I reasoned that a child with greater needs would be better served by having two parents, but the crude fact was I was not prepared to raise a child with certain disabilities. Every parent hopes for a healthy child, but there are millions of people raising children with severe mental and physical disabilities. There are no words to describe my admiration for these people and in stark contrast my own feelings of inadequacy, when I realised that I did not share their strength.

In addition, spending time with Sam and Oliver had taken on a new perspective as they were now competing for my attention. Any cuddles with the gorgeous babies came at the expense of my time with the older boys. I felt torn as I could not give either of them my undivided attention. I recognised that I had to be realistic as to my capabilities and the children's needs. So, after much soul searching and lengthy discussions with friends and family, I took the decision to apply to adopt one child.

My paperwork was now complete and my adoption application was due to go before a panel on Monday 1st July 2013.

Fortunately, I had precious little time to worry about the ultimate judgement day as my football team occupied the majority of my attention during the interim month. We had a series of important matches in quick succession and ultimately finished the season as league champions. Not surprisingly, the celebrations stretched into the early hours of the morning.

My reign as manager had been an incredible roller-coaster of unbelievable highs and stressful, time consuming lows. I had started the team from scratch, with nothing but a philosophy—that women should be able to enjoy playing football. I had been supported throughout by Whickham Fellside Youth Football Club and my good friend and stalwart assistant manager, Jen.

I took a step back in the crowded sports bar, watching the girls as they laughed and danced with their arms interlocked. A spirit of happiness and achievement shone among the synthetic smoke and disco lights. I had taken 15 strangers and formed a successful team, but watching that amazing group of women that night made me realise that it was the friendship and the camaraderie that gave me the greatest pride and satisfaction. The knowledge that I had created something so special was magical, but I had decided to step down, I needed to cut back on my commitments.

Adoption was now firmly on my horizon.

Twenty-Six

The panel date fell on my dayshift and it was the first time my adoption journey had clashed with my work. However, a phone call to the staffing officer unearthed an unexpected bonus—I was entitled to up to three days leave to attend necessary adoption meetings. I had heard the term 'family friendly' banded around the fire service, but I was now appreciating it for myself. The simple existence of a procedure created a sense of support.

The lads had regularly asked how the process was going, but home visits and information sessions meant very little to them. The panel was different, they recognised the enormity of the situation—the rest of my life depended on the outcome, and their support was palpable. I had started to imagine life as a parent, but I suppressed it as much as possible until I knew that the dream could come true.

I stared through the same door I had only 12 weeks ago, into the pale green room with its high ceilings and traditional wooden windows. The comfortable seats of the course had been stacked to one side and several desks made up a large rectangular table, around which a dozen people sat. My heart was beating fast and my mouth dried up, my clammy hands reached for the handle and I entered the old council office room for the most important job interview of my life.

The twelve people each introduced themselves, I was told their name and their role. In contrast, they had each read an 80-page document detailing every aspect of my life.

They asked questions pertaining to my report, ironing out any uncertainties. I only remember one question,

"Will you continue working shifts?"

It was something I had thought long and hard over, but I always came back to the same answer.

"To be honest, I don't know. I would hope to, but I've found it really difficult to imagine a child I've never met. I don't know their age or background and I cannot say for sure how they will settle and whether I could leave them overnight. I want to continue being a firefighter, but there are other options if I need them."

The panel nodded, aware of my time in the prevention and education department.

"But…" another question fired in, "would that be enough for you?"

It was a genuine concern. A child's placement could not be at the expense of my happiness.

"Yes, it would." I was sincere as I explained, "I joined the fire service to help people, but fire is destructive. As a firefighter, I respond to save lives and properties. It can be extremely rewarding, but also devastating. Even successful rescues can be accompanied by a ravaged family home. Releasing a casualty from a car collision is gratifying, but life-changing injuries can quickly invalidate any feeling of euphoria. Saving a stricken flood victim as sewage water submerges their memories, personal belongings and safe haven, cannot be described as satisfying. I've learned that there is a limit to what we can do and it's important to walk away, physically and mentally when we reach that point. However, I also realise that there are other ways to help people and preventing an accident can be equally rewarding."

"But would that be exciting enough for you?"

The questions were well meaning, asked without judgement and with the best possible intentions, but I could feel myself perspiring. The panel were leaning forward, like vultures over a carcass. This was evidently the biggest bone of contention and they were not letting up.

I sat back in my seat and looked around at each of them as I replied.

"I cannot imagine anything more exciting than being a parent, so if that is the extent of my excitement, I am more than happy with that."

The questions were wrapped up and I was asked to leave.

I waited downstairs with Melanie in a tiny office. There was only enough room for one of us to sit and she insisted that I did. My heart was still pumping fast, but the nervous butterflies had now fluttered away. I had done everything I could.

Thankfully, I didn't have to wait long before the Chair-lady appeared at the door. She was an affable woman in her early fifties with a professional nondescript expression, but she broke into a cheerful smile as she extended a hand.

"Congratulations, Kate. The decision was unanimous, your application has been approved!"

It was an amazing moment, a mix of relief and uncontrollable excitement. I could now start imagining myself as a parent. It was just a matter of waiting for a child to be matched with.

I thanked the two ladies who had made my dream a reality and as Melanie left to print off some documents, I happily considered who I should ring first.

As it happened, I didn't ring anyone. In fact, I barely spoke to another person for the next 24 hours. Melanie had returned to the room clutching a folder, containing the details of a child who was considered a suitable match. I had entered the building hoping the panel would approve my application and I could begin to plan for parenthood. I left an hour later with a file that filled me with exhilaration and fear. I had not prepared myself for this.

I sent a group text to all my family and friends saying that I had been approved and was over the moon. Then I put the file down on the passenger seat and drove home.

I didn't want to allow myself to get carried away, and I tried to give myself time to process the events of the day. It was amazing to get matched so soon, but there were no guarantees. I felt like I had just dipped my toe into a river and now I was being carried by the current. I was enjoying the ride, but it happened so fast I couldn't tell if I was meant to be coming this way.

Throughout the adoption course I had learned an enormous amount. However, I now realised that I had absolutely no idea how I was supposed to feel after seeing a black and white account of a child's life. It was a necessarily clinical analysis and simply produced the facts, but I felt uneasy. The report described a little boy, Shaun, who was 22 months old. Social workers and health visitors had remarked that he was healthy and developing well. There was nothing to suggest he had any of the conditions that were apparently prevalent in children who come into care. I was the luckiest woman alive, I had hit the jackpot. However, I was devastated because it didn't feel like it.

I read the report several times over and each time tried to picture the little boy who was being portrayed. He sounded perfect—a happy toddler who loved swimming, soft play and being outdoors. If I was to handpick my perfect child, it would have been him. Shaun was not the problem. I was—my lack of reaction didn't seem normal.

I wanted to talk it through with someone and Chris was the obvious choice. He had been there before and I could rely on him to be honest. I asked Chris to read the report which he did, thoroughly. He then looked up and said,

"It looks like you've hit lucky."

"I know, he sounds perfect."

Chris looked confused. I continued,

"It sounds a little too perfect, so I wanted you to check I hadn't missed anything."

Chris looked back down at the report.

"No, it all looks really straightforward." He paused. "You don't seem too sure."

"I'm not, Chris, that's the problem. I didn't have an immediate realisation that this child would be my son and I don't love him. I don't even know if we would get on."

Chris smiled and simply said, "I would have been worried if you did."

From then on, I relaxed and trusted my own feelings rather than trying to force something that was not there. When Melanie called and asked if I wanted to proceed and find out more information I said 'yes'. When she asked for my initial thoughts, I said 'he seemed great'. I wanted to keep it low key. I had only read fundamental details about Shaun. Factual information regarding his age, height, weight, likes and dislikes, cannot bring a child to life.

As we filtered into work the next morning, my watch ambushed me for news, but I wanted to let Ray know first. I explained the situation in his office and he looked as shocked as me.

"Oh, right...okay..." There was not much he could say. It was an awkward set of circumstances.

I was walking a tightrope of emotions and struggling to find the balance. I was mentally preparing myself for impending motherhood. The joy and responsibility were overwhelming, but I needed to protect myself from the possible heartbreak of having it all ripped away.

Over the coming weeks I would learn more about the young boy who could become my son. I was undeniably excited, but I also became increasingly appreciative of my current life. I hadn't fully realised what I had until I was in danger of losing it.

Firefighting is not in my blood. I cannot identify the most significant aspects of my career in the physical world, but it resides in my soul. I am inexorably tied to a role that has given me so much. It is electrifying. The adrenaline rush, the unknown, the chance. Choices matter and decisions have the ultimate consequences. The exhilaration cannot be replicated.

During the early summer months of 2013, I treasured every incident, from false alarms to persons reported. Every emergency call and every ride in a fire engine could be my last. I savoured the 22:00 hour film, the drills, the banter and the mundane work routine. My job was integral to who I was—my social life revolved round shift patterns, my gym motivation was intricately linked to being able to fulfil my role and I would identify myself as a firefighter above any-thing else. The thought of leaving it all behind forever ter-rified me.

A visit from Shaun's social worker and foster carer brought the pages of his report to life. I listened intently as his foster carer described a delightful little character with a big personality and a loving heart. In many ways a typical boy, who loved being active and was a very happy, settled child. I sympathised with her, her love for Shaun was evident. A move would be traumatic for both of them.

As they talked, I could feel my chest swell with affection, Shaun had already occupied a place in my heart. I was given a photograph and when they left 90 minutes later, I placed it in various parts of my house, trying to imagine him being there. It was surreal—that red-haired blue-eyed boy with the cheeky smile could be my son.

I was now desperate for the match to go ahead, but I had to wait until Melanie called to give me the verdict. I sat on the stairs, with a look that resembled a toddler's first glimpse of soft play as I was told the foster carer and social worker had agreed that the child and I would be a good match. Everything now depended on the outcome of the next panel meeting. It was set for two weeks' time—Monday, 5th August, 2013.

It was a strange passage of time. On one hand, motherhood was tantalisingly close and I ardently wanted to meet Shaun, but on the other hand I was passionately clinging to work. I wasn't ready to say goodbye.

The summer months saw an increase in grass fires. They were often several hundred metres from the nearest road, making access and water supply difficult. On my last night shift of a busy set we received one such call at 03:00 hours.

There was no immediate risk and we were out in the crisp, clear, unspoilt air of the dead of night. I loved these jobs. We travelled along the riverside, with the windows down. Despite a lack of visible evidence, we could smell the beautiful earthly aroma of a pure burn. The smoke from fires involving tyres, plastics and metal is menacingly thick and black, with an acrid taste that sticks to the back of your throat, but natural fuel was different—innocent and homely, I savoured it.

It became evident that the scent was drifting from the south side of the river, but our appliance exceeded the weight limit of the bridge. Using another crossing would take several minutes and we would only get marginally closer to the fire. So, we parked up and while the driver waited with the truck, three of us set off, armed with beaters, shovels and as much water as we could carry.

We took torches, but we walked comfortably in moonlight for ten minutes before we saw the smoke rise from the moorland.

Conserving our water, we beat the grass fire into submission. It had spread to a nearby fence and the timber frames were stubborn in their resistance. Water was the only viable option, but we were satisfied the fire was completely extinguished when the last drop of our supply was exhausted.

We were ready to leave when a defiant glow of orange shone from the trunk of a neighbouring tree. Using the shovel, we scraped away at the bark and the burning section, but the smouldering wood was too far ingrained to have much effect. We needed more water. It would be another 30 minutes graft for the smallest of embers. Furthermore, the earth was so dry, a tiny spark could set the whole area alight in the same timeframe.

Our enthusiasm drained. Wasting time was a common bugbear amongst firefighters. Despondent, we gathered our equipment.

"Hang on a minute." It was Billy, our crew manager.

Billy's dark crewcut and tanned, crease-free face, belied science. He was in his fifties, but could easily pass for a 30-year old. I reasoned it was his laid-back attitude and his simplistic black and white take on life. He appeared to have very few cares in the world.

We stopped.

"Kate, turn around will you," he was fumbling with his fly.

I had been to many incidents, especially in my early career, which had given rise to the line 'you could piss on that!" Most memorably, when we called to put out a pizza box on fire in the middle of a car park. On that occasion, it was thrown into a puddle. Call challenging was now undertaken in the control room, the operators syphoned out hoax callers and ridiculous requests. It had had the desired effect and reduced wasteful use of our resources, but it placed a great deal of additional responsibility on the control room operators. It can be virtually impossible to decipher between a drunk nuisance caller and a distressed individual who may slur their words due to a medical condition.

Nevertheless, that night, Billy did what others only spoke of, and thanks to his bladder and ingenuity, the fire was now completely out.

Adapt. Improvise. Overcome.

The unofficial motto from the United States Marine Corps was widely used in the fire service. Our training could not account for every scenario and the slogan fitted with our basic approach—if it doesn't work, try something else. I have adopted this rudimentary approach in my home life and found it incredibly liberating. It unburdens every task from the notion of perfection or failure, and champions a way forward. With the prospect of motherhood beckoning, there was no better time to reinforce the message.

I dawdled out of the station that morning. I was about to start my annual leave—whatever happened at the panel meeting, I had 21 glorious days off ahead of me, but if the match was approved, there was a chance I would not be back. My life was no longer entirely on my own terms and my child's wellbeing, happiness and security had to come before anything else. No-one was able to accurately predict how well he would settle or whether he could cope with being left in the care of someone else. Some of the adoptees who had spoken at our information sessions had explained how they had left work to accommodate their child's need for stability. I didn't know if he'd be able to manage a day at a nursery, let alone a night at a stranger's house.

Ordinarily, my attendance at the matching panel would have been compulsory, but on August 5th, 2013, I was in the South of France, at the wedding of two of my closest friends, Jen and Laura. A month had passed since I had been approved as a prospective adopter by the same group of people, and I was still fresh in their minds. It was therefore decided that Melanie, as my adoption worker, could attend on my behalf.

She phoned through with some questions from the panel.

"Which member of your family has red hair?"

"What?!" I was panicking, my heart felt like it was pumping in my throat. My friends turned towards me, searching for news. No-one in my family had red hair. I hadn't foreseen it as an issue and I couldn't believe my dreams were going to be torn apart by the colour of my hair. The mobile reception was poor and I was bouncing from one side of the villa to the other.

"No-one. Is that really going to be a problem? I'll dye my hair if necessary."

Melanie was completely unruffled, even as we spoke, thousands of miles apart, I could sense her professional composure. "Don't worry, Kate, the very fact they are asking it means they are struggling for questions, it's a good sign."

I breathed out and instantly felt calmer.

I tried to relax, but I stared at my phone and refused to go into the swimming pool until I had heard back from Melanie.

Thirty minutes later, sitting on a sun lounger in Provence, in my favourite attire of board shorts and clutching an ice-cold beer, I discovered that I was going to be a mum. I was elated and grabbed another beer with friends to celebrate. As I lay there, soaking up the sun and absorbing my life changing news, I was blissfully unaware that I was enjoying my last totally chilled out moment.

Twenty-Seven

Nothing prepares you for parenthood.

It was a standard line, spewed by virtually every parent as they congratulate a new arrival. I knew that no amount of organisation could prime me for the most dramatic transformation of my life. However, I had not accounted for being so tremendously underprepared.

I arrived home on Saturday August 10th, to a house without a kitchen. Back in the spring of 2013, there had been no urgency and I seized on an opportunity to get the majority of the work done while I was on holiday.

Mark from the blue watch had done a fantastic job installing my new bathroom, and the kitchen was beginning to take shape. He had four days of firefighting ahead of him, but assured me that everything would be squared away on Thursday and Friday.

I was nodding away, but couldn't contain my excitement.

"My little guy will be coming home soon!"

"Bloody hell, Kate!" Mark looked from the newly

plastered ceilings and walls, down to the partially tiled floor. "When?!"

I had no prior experience and yet I announced with confidence, "Oh, it won't be until the end of next week. I have a meeting on Thursday to discuss the introductions. They will probably start on Monday and I guess he will move a week after that." I smiled, feeling guilty for causing unnecessary stress. "I have plenty of time"

I was wrong.

Introductions are carefully managed and every case is different, but as a general rule, the younger the child is the shorter the introductory period. The reason being that babies and toddlers would find a prolonged ricochet between primary carers confusing, whereas older children would need the time to adapt. We were told to expect a week's introductions for every year of the child's life. Shaun was 22 months, so I inferred it would be a week to ten days. In hindsight, I was embarrassed at my ignorance when I presumed the meetings to start on a Monday. Social Workers and foster carers were not routine occupations and there was little sense in delaying a child's arrival at their forever home. However, when I assembled with Melanie, the adoption manager and Shaun's foster carer on Thursday 15th August, to discuss the series of visits that would culminate in him coming home, I had no idea that I would be meeting my son three hours later.

I was desperate to meet Shaun, and on the 60-minute drive I pictured the instant connection as our eyes met for the first time. My heart would fill with love for the son I was destined to have and every cell in my body would melt as he wrapped his arms around me and whispered "Mummy". However, as I neared Shaun's foster home, I exited the A1 and entered reality.

I was terrified that Shaun and I would not connect or even like each other. I was sweating and struggling to breathe. It felt like butterflies were leaving my stomach and lodging in my throat. I was choking in anticipation.

As I parked up alongside the house, I caught my first glimpse of Shaun through the window. He was looking out, his bright red hair barely visible over the window sill, but he was out of focus—my eyes were filling up.

I didn't need to knock, the door opened and I was ushered in. I acknowledged Zara, Shaun's social worker, before peering round the door to see my son properly for the first time.

He grinned shyly in acknowledgement before bouncing around—perfectly content to perform for his audience, but from a distance he was comfortable with. I sat down next to Zara who produced a book from her bag and sparked Shaun's curiosity. He stood between us and placed a hand on my knee. That slightest touch meant the world to me.

That first visit went brilliantly. Shaun laughed hysterically as I blew bubbles for him and then grabbed a book and settled himself on my knee. I drove back up the A1 high on adrenaline.

Over the coming days, I worked on building a rapport

with Shaun, but I was finding the introductions difficult. Louise, Shaun's foster carer, was visibly affected and as her voice wavered, I felt an incredible burden of responsibility. There were so many contradictions—I wanted to love, but I didn't want to force it. I wanted to feel elated, but in truth I was scared.

I had heard adoptive parents say that they knew immediately from reading the details that their child was right for them and that they fell in love the second they set eyes on them. It sounds idyllic and romantic, but that isn't how it happened for me. As much as I would have loved it to, perpetuating the fairy tale would be damaging and untrue. Despite the fact I was desperate to, I had absolutely no idea if I was going to love Shaun.

It was an extremely difficult situation, because I wanted him. I wanted to take him home and learn to love him. However, that want was teamed with fear and guilt. What if I could not love him? What if he would be better off with someone else, someone who loved him the moment they set eyes on him?

My days were a whirlwind. I struggled to manage my emotions, the two-hour commute to Shaun's foster home and an intense redecorating schedule. I was running on adrenaline and had very little time to process my feelings, Shaun's needs and every practicality. I had to focus entirely on each exact moment. If I allowed my mind to wander, the enormity of the situation was in danger of swallowing me up.

Shaun's traumatic early life had caused selective mutism. He was in many ways a typical toddler, swinging from extreme emotions. However, while his foster parents were able to read his non-verbal cues and intercept his temper triggers, I was flying blind.

Fortunately, it was Shaun's unique method of communication that ultimately gave me the strength and reassurance I needed.

On the third day of introductions, we went on our first solo outing. I was enjoying the opportunity to get to know Shaun away from his foster carers, chasing him through a soft play as he giggled excitedly. After 45 minutes of crawling around, I had decided to force myself through a tunnel that was clearly designed to embarrass any adult foolish enough to give it a go. Like a butterfly emerging from a cocoon, my top half was free when I caught Shaun's wonderful blue eyes. I stopped struggling and held his stare. Then he gave me a cheeky smile, leaned forward and kissed me.

I savoured our surreal private moment. Time seemed to stand still and my heart pounded with joy. However, an angry shout from a child behind brought me back to reality and I wriggled myself clear.

Later that evening, I was sitting with Louise and her husband, watching Shaun's bedtime routine so I could replicate it and ease his transition. Fresh from bathing and lathered in eczema cream, Shaun played contentedly beneath the window. It was his wind down time and I watched him from the furthest point of the room. I was there to observe, not interfere.

Shaun's foster carers were watching him too—their love for him was palpable.

We chatted comfortably about routines, likes and dislikes as I tried to glean as much information as I could, but Shaun's cry pierced the conversation.

He was rubbing his head and searching for a cuddle. I offered a sympathetic smile, but remained seated. I was counting down the days till Shaun would come home, but for now I had to face facts—Louise had been Shaun's primary carer for ten months, she was his safe place and the one person he would naturally seek out for comfort and reassurance. She leant forward with arms outstretched ready to scoop him up, but to my amazement, Shaun walked straight to me. As he reached up with both arms, his wet eyes bursting with love and trust, everything stilled—even my heart appeared to stop beating. I wrapped him in my arms and he nestled contentedly on my lap. I cannot adequately describe the feeling in words. It was a moment that made me realise this was exactly where I was supposed to be. Firefighting, my dreams of promotion and ideas of exotic travel all paled into insignificance as I realised my life's purpose was resting sleepily on my knee.

There were many times over the coming months when the enormity of motherhood overwhelmed me. Indulging in self-doubt and drowning in fear, I would sit on the stairs listening to the screams of a boy I could not understand. Head in hands I would recall the instant that my son showed absolute confidence that his hopes and dreams were safe in my hands. I drew strength from his conviction and vowed that I would not let him down.

Five days after we met, having spent less than twenty-four hours in each-others company, 22-month old Shaun came home on Tuesday, 20th August. He coped remarkably well and I crammed in as many activities as possible, but tears filled his eyes at bedtime and my heart ached as he silently acknowledged a profound sense of loss before he drifted off to sleep.

Shaun moved in before my three weeks of leave were over. It had been a tumultuous 21 days—the amazing week in France had been followed by meeting my son, as well as redecorating and preparing the house for his arrival. I had not given the fire service a second thought until I realised that I had forgotten to apply for the necessary adoption leave. Fortunately, the human resources department granted my request for twelve months off work.

During the adoption process, an extended settling in period was recommended and a year seemed standard. However, in reality each placement was unique and the time off work could be adapted according to the child and the circumstances of the family. I naively thought of it as a holiday—it was anything but.

The first week was a dream. It was just Shaun and I—family and friends could be introduced over the coming weeks, but Shaun needed time to build an attachment to me without the distraction of others. I was driven by excitement and idealistic thoughts, and Shaun was a perfect child. He did everything I asked, slept for 14 hours a day and never cried once. I did not realise the poor little guy was too traumatised to do much else. It took a while for Shaun's infantile brain to process that his whole world had been turned upside down.

I was hyper. My experience of children had been as a fun aunt, and I was adopting the same high-octane approach with Shaun—cramming in as many activities and trips to the park as possible. After a week, Shaun's anger and resentment erupted. High-pitched screaming was accompanied by a fierce pounding of his hands and legs. My little boy had been uprooted, pulled from everything he loved and everyone who made him feel safe. His rage was an entirely legitimate manifestation of his distress and hurt. However, as the stress of the last few weeks caught up with me, I began to interpret Shaun lashing out as a personal attack and I questioned my abilities and suitability for the job. I was beat, entirely spent and struggling to function. Overnight I had gone from a single, carefree woman to a full time mum. Now the innocent enthusiasm that drives new adventures had slipped away and I mourned the loss of my previous life.

My thoughts left me crippled with compunction. I was failing an innocent toddler, his foster carers, social workers and birth parents. I had promised him a good life, filled with love and laughs, and I had nosedived spectacularly.

As the weeks passed, I survived countless lonely nights accompanied only by the enduring guilt of parenthood and the persistent feeling of inadequacy. Days began too soon and became a feat of endurance interspersed by inane conversations with perfect parents and the angry screams of a boy I did not yet know.

Still, I found myself repeating a mantra passed down by parents since the beginning of time,

"It is the best thing I have ever done."

It wasn't true—I had an infinite list of things that were better than my isolated existence, devoid of sleep and excitement, but I feared any deviation would highlight a weakness in my maternal make up. I felt as if I had fallen for the greatest lie ever told and dutifully maintained the secret, not for the sake of mankind, but for the purpose of reeling friends into the abyss.

When Jen and Laura returned from honeymoon, I laid it on thick.

"It's amazing guys, honestly. Shaun has made my life complete. He's a proper little character!"

That bit was true, Shaun had an amazing personality and an infectious laugh that bellowed across a room. His emotions were extreme. I was not comfortable being the centre of attention, but Shaun threw us both into the limelight. He was intent on doing his own thing regardless of what was expected. As the other children complied perfectly at 'Gym Tots', Shaun would spend the hour running riot. I chased after him and took every opportunity to tell other parents that I had just adopted him.

The football team were short for Sunday's game and

Laura was nursing an injury. She offered to look after Shaun if I agreed to play. I jumped at the opportunity, loving the sense of freedom and the connection to my old life.

It was a brilliant, timely reminder that I could make things work. I didn't have to sacrifice everything now I was a mum.

As Shaun settled in, we were able to see other people and travel further than the local park. I felt calmer as our world opened up. Shaun was an adventurous and inquisitive little boy and the initial settling in period was difficult for us both. I understood it was important for us to form a relationship and for Shaun to feel comfortable in his new surroundings. It had been a necessary but fractious start and I was pleased it was behind us.

A few days later, I introduced Shaun to the concept of 'napping' and rejoiced as he dozed. The simple act allowed us both an opportunity to relax. The time we spent together became enjoyable rather than endurable. I celebrated every tiny success as a beacon of hope; every cuddle, every gesture I could understand, every meal he ate was a step forward. The journey was extremely difficult. It was excruciatingly lonely, mentally draining, physically exhausting and infinitely daunting. Yet that passage of time saw us travel from complete strangers to becoming a mother and son, and consequently became the most rewarding and inspiring of my life.

Twenty-Eight

Shaun and I had been regular visitors to the station throughout my adoption leave. He would shriek in delight as he pretended to drive the fire engines, soaking up the attention as the lads fussed over him. I enjoyed the connection—my son and my vocation existing in perfect harmony. My dream of combining motherhood and fire-fighting was tangibly close.

Four months after Shaun came home, we celebrated a magical first Christmas together and joined the rest of my family at my parents' home for lunch. A year ago, I had announced that I was going to apply to adopt around this very table and here I was with my son. I couldn't imagine life without him.

However, as a new year began, I also couldn't shake the feeling that Shaun and I were living in an unsustainable bubble, and a gnawing fear increasingly took hold. The thought of returning to work began to consume me.

Undeniably I missed the excitement, the banter and the lads. I craved the intensity and the unknown—an episode of Peppa Pig and a marathon swing pushing session could not conjure the same appeal. Ultimately, however, the main driving force behind my urgency to return to work was my fear of failure.

Working parents everywhere testify to the difficulties of juggling childcare with a career. I saw it as the pinnacle—the ultimate test and measure of whether I would succeed as a parent. My attachment to Shaun was growing with every passing day. To preserve his home and to keep his world secure, I needed to work and the thought of letting him down terrified me. I could not bear the wait, I needed to know if I was capable. So, in February 2014, I began to make arrangements to return to the fire service.

Shaun's Adoption Order was still eight weeks away, so I didn't yet have full parental responsibility. While it was shared with the local authority, Melanie and Zara would visit periodically. It was an opportunity to communicate any concerns and to monitor Shaun's transition. I talked through my plans and welcomed their input.

I second guessed myself endlessly and craved affirmation that I was doing the right thing. As Shaun slept, I would pour myself a glass of red wine and spend several hours googling answers to questions I agonised over. However, it was a ridiculous waste of time as I merely scrolled through until I found a response that supported my viewpoint. I had imagined many perils of single parenting—the loneliness, the constant juggling of tasks, the fact that you could not give yourself time out, but it was the sole responsibility that I struggled with most. The idea that every decision fell exclusively to me.

Shaun had been moved so many times in his young life, he needed consistency and I could not afford to get it wrong. I questioned whether it was too soon, if he was ready to be separated from me, whether he trusted that I would come back for him, whether he would settle, be happy and all of the other considerations that working parents wrestle with. However, at the same time, I wanted him to have more interaction with people and develop socially.

When I watched Shaun play, I saw a gorgeous, happy boy, with an infinite capacity for love. His wide eyes and ruddy cheeks glowed with positivity as he charged at full speed into everything that life had to offer, but my heart ached as I sensed the inevitable inner turmoil and confusion in my little boy's head. A toddler brain processing a sense of loss that would flaw most adults. Two months before his second birthday he was removed from everything he knew and everything that made him feel safe. It was the fourth time Shaun had needed to start over. Each time his carer had expected him to withdraw and protect himself against another upheaval, but the tiny redhead exhibited a resilience and strength that belied his age, and seemingly adjusted to every new chapter in his life with the ease of a chameleon. Nevertheless, I was mindful of the accumulative effect and I had a constant fear that every new change could be one too many.

It was imperative that Shaun was eased through the

transition of my return to work and I decided to implement one change at a time. I would introduce Shaun to a day nursery first and return to the Prevention and Education department. When I was happy Shaun had settled, I could look to introduce night shifts.

Newburn Riverside Co-operative Nursery was the second nursery I visited. I had dragged Shaun kicking and screaming from The Little Cubs only minutes earlier and he was still furious with me when we pulled up outside. Dreading a repeat performance, I entered the doors with the same resigned acceptance as a visit to the dentist.

Fortunately, Shaun and I fell in love with the whole set up, from the staff to the extensive outdoor play area. Furthermore, the long-term availability was flexible and I was reassured that they could accommodate my shifts. Shaun settled amazingly well at nursery and instantly formed a close bond with Jasmine, a young woman with bright red hair as vibrant as her personality. She loved and understood Shaun on every level, and the affection she had for him was genuine—enthusing over every tiny achievement, laughing at every mishap and celebrating every milestone. Shaun deserved that kind of love. My family loved him, but our visits were sporadic. Jasmine provided a regular support for Shaun which diffused the intensity of our relationship. He was settled and happy. His speech developed steadily and many of his frustrations melted away. I was back working with Ben, juggling a son and a career. Shaun was blossoming and I was thriving as a single parent. I had successfully negotiated the hurdle I had dreaded the most and it was incredibly empowering.

However, there remained a nagging void.

I felt like a child swinging across hanging bars, in that momentum is essential in getting to the next rung. The longer I stayed in the Prevention and Education department, the harder it would be to leave. The job was safe and the hours were flexible. In many respects, it was the perfect role for a single parent, but I missed life on a watch.

Without exception, my family and friends thought I was crazy and I was repeatedly told that I had to put Shaun's needs ahead of my own.

However, I don't see a parent and child's needs as mutually exclusive. I want Shaun to fight for his dreams, to go after them with everything he has, and I do not believe surrendering my own aspirations would set a very good example. Shaun is a major consideration in every decision I make, but we are a team and our emotions are intricately entwined—neither of us would be truly happy if it was at the expense of the other. Furthermore, the shifts would allow Shaun and I to spend more time together. The current arrangement meant we had two days off together, but Shaun would be tired, grumpy and invariably poorly by the time the weekend rolled round.

"Yes, but that's the same as everyone else. Everybody is in the same boat. You just have to get used to it."

I can't attribute the line to any individual. It was a common vein of thought, permeating virtually every section of my social circle, but it infuriated me.

I recognise that 9-5 remains the undisputed norm of working hours, and I realise that it suits lots of people. However, it wasn't the life I wanted. I didn't feel it necessary to submit to the faceless mass of society or comply with unwritten rules of what was expected. I had sacrificed happiness and fulfilment at work for comfort and security, but I was spending very little quality time with my son. I was existing, treading water, but I wanted more.

I found a childminder, Jo, who would have Shaun overnight and he would continue at the nursery for my day shifts. My childcare arrangements were comprehensive and would cover the time I was due to be at work, but they were far from robust and I was concerned that I could not account for every scenario—what if I got called out to an incident and could not pick Shaun up in time? What if he was ill and I was at a job? What if Shaun was poorly and I needed to stay off with him?

As a firefighter, I cannot account for every possible scenario. My colleagues and I take risks and push every safety margin to the limit. However, there are times when you just have to hope that things will work out.

I viewed motherhood in the same vein and resolved that I would not be discouraged by a series of hypothetical situations. I finally returned to the White Watch in August 2014, twelve months after I had left the station to commence my annual leave.

I was nervous but exhilarated to be back working as a

firefighter. I loved being back amongst the lads, in a team and with a purpose. There had been some considerable changes in both equipment and procedures and I felt like a stranger among pieces of kit that had once felt so familiar. However, after two days of training I was ready to take my place on a fire engine for the night shifts.

I had a knot in my stomach from the moment I woke up and struggled all day with a sense of dread. I looked at Shaun and felt selfish. He was a small, vulnerable young boy who needed stability, and I was packing him off to stay with someone he barely knew so I could do the job I wanted. Once again, Shaun silenced my doubts as he dragged his little trunki fire engine suitcase down the stairs and declared himself ready a full three hours before we needed to leave.

Shaun adapted remarkably well to his new routine. He spent my day shifts with Jasmine at the nursery and on night shifts he slept at Jo's house. He was welcomed and treated as one of Jo's family and he loved his evenings there. I had been concerned that he would be unsettled, but I came to realise that the opposite had occurred—by leaving Shaun and coming back for him, I was reinforcing the message that I would always be there. Furthermore, by opening up Shaun's world, I was inviting more people to love him and that could only be a good thing.

I loved being back and I savoured every aspect of the job—the smell of fire, the calls and the ambiguity, the conversations, the gym and the interaction with the public. I enjoyed the familiar banter with the lads, the combined focus on a task and the sense of inclusion. In many ways, it was as if I had never been away.

Shift work granted Shaun and I more time together. I felt fulfilled and happy. I was blissfully content and my emotions resonated in my son. I was living my dream. There were inevitably many moments of anguish and our new arrangement did not come without its pitfalls—I would pace the station in the final thirty minutes of every shift, praying we did not get overtime, searching for a colleague who could 'jump' for me—a firefighter who would take my place on the appliance for the last few minutes of a shift, minimising my risk of working beyond Shaun's nursery hours. However, without fail, I collected Shaun on time.

Then Shaun contracted chickenpox. The spots first appeared during my second nightshift, but Jo was happy for him to stay the night. I collected him the next morning and had four days off to nurse him.

On the fifth day, I was due back at work, but by a happy coincidence, Laura was enjoying a few days off in between jobs and offered to look after Shaun. I dropped him at my friend's house before I started work.

I was detached to a neighbouring station, driving a hugely likeable officer in charge. Barry was well intentioned, but had an unfortunate habit of engaging his mouth before his brain. His watch loved him and had repeatedly encouraged him to postpone his retirement. Equally, I found Barry endearingly eccentric and we had a good working relationship.

Barry had served almost his entire 30 years in a completely male environment and as he guided me round his station area, he steered the conversation onto female firefighters. We were still something of an enigma to him. The sisterhood's numbers had swelled from 3 to 20 during my time in the brigade—spectacularly failing to meet the government target of 15% of the workforce. I knew a handful of them from football, a few others from passing at incidents or in a locker room, but I did not know any of them well enough to pass comment as to their abilities as a firefighter. Barry however, confidently judged every single one of them. There were not enough of us to merit the conversation lasting more than a couple of minutes; it would have fizzled out, but Barry put his own indelible stamp on it,

"Well, I tell you something Kate. I would not have a female firefighter driving me."

A stunned silence descended on the cab as we each took a second to ascertain if we had heard correctly. I glanced across at Barry; he was deep in thought and oblivious to his faux pas. My eyes scrunched in disbelief and darted back to the road. Like a boxer, absorbing a punch, I shook my head and moved on. However, the lads could not let the moment pass without insults and laughter streaming through from the back.

"Barry, man! You can't say that!"

The guilty party suddenly caught up.

'Oh… I did not mean YOU, Kate. YOU can drive me any day!'

I could not take offence. The poor guy spent the rest of the shift bombarding me with compliments. In many ways, I was grateful that I was still seen as one of the team following my adoption leave and a self-imposed exile in the office. However, Barry's words were an infuriating reminder that some managers were so blinded by the term 'female fire-fighter' that they couldn't see the individual. The parochialism was suffocating, but I refused to be drawn in. Mother-hood had undoubtedly changed me.

I no longer cared what others thought of me. Shaun permeated my every thought. My son's well-being was all that mattered.

The following day, Shaun was no longer contagious and allowed back into nursery. I had negotiated another stumbling block without any impact on my job. I've found that events and circumstances often work to my favour if I'm prepared to push boundaries and explore the limits of my capabilities. Admittedly, there were flaws in my childcare arrangements, but miraculously, it worked.

My new cavalier attitude was incredibly liberating. I now recognised the need to focus my energy on the aspects of my life that I could influence. I was not going to change long standing beliefs held by a powerful minority of individuals within the fire service.

From the day I started, without exception, the lads I worked with were brilliant and loyal, testifying to my worth and dispelling myths. Yet, completely fabricated stories concerning me and other female firefighters continued to be a toxic poison—on one occasion an account of my detachment to another station was doing the rounds, the story was that I had been asked to wash up and I categorically refused, spraying expletives around like confetti and explaining, "I don't wash up at my own station, so there's no way I'm doing it here!"

The 'meek' members of that particular watch had been so taken aback that they apparently scrambled a cup of tea together in the hope it would calm me down.

In truth I had barely exchanged two words throughout that noteworthy detachment. I was a solitary figure on parade until the watch manager arrived and explained that his crew did not like working with women. I checked my breathing apparatus set and the equipment alone and made every attempt to ingratiate myself with the group by doing everything for them. I recognised it was futile, but I mulishly removed ammunition from people desperate to have a go.

Nevertheless, their version infiltrated every branch of the brigade. I cannot deny that it hurt. However, something unexpected was happening—people were sticking up for me. I understood that it was easier to stay quiet and go with the incessant flow of mess room banter. I realised that most firefighters and managers had no issues with the female contingent and would simply let the stories pass over them, but now firefighters throughout the brigade were speaking out on our behalf and creating a new story in itself. It was both humbling and empowering.

There was a tangible sense that the tide was turning,

female firefighters were finally approaching a genuine parity with our male counterparts.

I should have been euphoric, but there was an ominous dark cloud nestled over fire stations throughout the country. We were in the midst of another strike.

Twenty-Nine

The fierce opposition to the increased retirement age had several layers of discontent. I signed up to the 1992 Firefighters Pension Scheme on my very first day at training school. I could barely afford the payments that equated to an eighth of my pay, but it meant I would get my 30-year pension at the age of 53 and I made the decision that it was a sacrifice worth making. I doubted that as a female approaching my mid-fifties, I would be capable of remaining operationally fit, but as a wide-eyed recruit I aspired to work up the chain of command and did not believe I would still be riding fire engines. However, in 2015, fifteen years into my career, a vocation I had no intention of leaving, I was told that the agreement was no longer applicable. I would have to work until I was 60. A promise was revoked and my planned future thrown into disarray.

Fire kit is designed to protect the wearer from fire. It doesn't contain a breathable membrane or high-tech cooling mechanism. It's worn in temperatures exceeding 800 degrees, where in natural circumstances your body starts chemically breaking down due to the heat. While working in this inhospitable atmosphere you are essentially blind, but lives depend on you finding them. You may be carrying equipment in excess of 30 kg and your heart rate soars from the exertion and sheer adrenaline. You could remain in this state for 20-30 minutes before you find a casualty possibly weighing in excess of 200 lbs because fires do not just kill lean people. The inevitable decline of physical fitness will unquestionably diminish a firefighter's ability, yet there are serving members that are due to retire in their mid-seventies.

It's a nonsensical scenario. The role does not allow for it. Firefighters would never allow a situation where lives are lost due to their fitness and ability to do the job required of them. However, the alternative is to leave the job and the pension they have invested so heavily in. A firefighter's skill set is unique to the post. Saving lives and putting out fires are not considered transferable skills and do not sit well in the modern world of recruitment. I was fearful as to the future of both the British Fire Service and the firefighters who continuously risk their lives for others. We began a series of discontinuous strikes on 3rd October 2013 in a desperate effort to protect the future we were promised and a right to see out our working life in the fire service.

Shaun and I had attended the picket lines sporadically throughout my adoption leave. It was a struggle that would drag on for years. Ultimately, the 2015 Firefighter Pension Scheme came into force, bringing an end to the striking action. Much like the 2002 strike, it had all been in vain.

Morale was notably low. The financial and emotional hardship of industrial action had been accentuated by a lack of belief. There was a tangible tone of resigned acceptance. We were fighting with our hearts, a love of the fire service and a conviction that the public deserved a first-class service. We took an enormous amount of pride in our work and trained hard to maintain fitness levels because we knew that it mattered. However, we were drowned out by an argument solely focused on money. Sadly, decisions appeared to be taken with no appreciation as to our actual role.

When I returned to work, following adoption leave, friends had joked that it would be like a holiday after several months of single parenting. It was good humoured and well-intentioned. However, firefighters were increasingly subjected to an unfair stereotype. Yes, we watched films on a night shift, we had access to the gym and we could sleep from midnight. Those are the aspects of our job that we are comfortable sharing with others. Very few incidents are ever reported to the press, either on the grounds of respect or ongoing investigations, and firefighters themselves will rarely speak of them.

We were conducting a routine inspection of a fish and chips premises when we got the call. A bus had collided with a motorcyclist on a country road several miles away. Our specialist appliance had been requested as it carries high pressure airbags and equipment capable of dealing with heavier vehicles. However, we did not have enough firefighters to staff both appliances. I drove back to the fire station on blue lights and there was a mad scramble to move our fire kit from one appliance to the other. The exchange was completed in minimal time, but it had cost us vital minutes.

The crews at the scene were desperate and we received repeated requests via control for our estimated arrival time.

My officer in charge looked across at me. I barely knew him. He had been detached in from Sunderland to cover a shortfall in our crew. He had little knowledge of the equipment carried on our specialist appliance or the local area.

"Five minutes," I told him, knowing I was being extremely optimistic.

As I negotiated the seemingly endless country lanes, I was acutely aware that every second would feel like a lifetime to the firefighters desperately trying to save the motorcyclists life. I wanted to give them hope. In the same tone, I left the sirens on, even when the roads were clear. The crews at the scene would appreciate that we were getting closer.

My hands gripped the steering wheel as my heart raced with the appliance. I could feel the hairs on the back of my neck. I was straining every sinew to maximise my speed. Concentrating entirely on the road, I took advantage of the low hedge line, checking for oncoming traffic and predicting each turn in the road. The cab was silent. I could sense the guys willing me through the speed barrier, mentally taking every bend with me.

At last we caught sight of the flashing blue lights. The police and ambulance were already in attendance along with our brothers and sisters.

"It's ok," I reassured my officer in charge as I scrambled down from my cab. "We've got this."

There was no pomp or ceremony, everyone did whatever was necessary. He climbed down and joined me at the locker, but a third person stepped between us.

"Kate."

It was a firefighter from a neighbouring station.

That single word, used as a greeting, told me everything.

It was the tone of his voice. The slow, deliberate manner he put his hands on the locker. The fact his eyes kept flitting to the ground.

The motorcyclist had been declared dead. It was now a recovery operation.

The atmosphere changed immediately—the intense determination, frenzied activity and heart rate ceased in a beat. My heart now appeared laboriously sluggish, people moved in slow motion, gathering in small groups.

Amongst our emergency service colleagues, firefighters are sometimes referred to as water fairies for obvious reasons, or daffodils—given our yellow helmets and the fact we hang round in bunches. I recognised that it rang true. I did seek refuge and comfort in familiarity and closeness. I valued our unity and shared experiences, in contrast I felt for the police officers and paramedics who often turned up alone.

The scene was quiet, sombre. There was little that could be said—few conversations fit comfortably in an atmosphere of recent death. Instead we become immersed in our own thoughts as we reran the last ten minutes on a constant loop. I scrutinized my every move from the moment we got the call. On this occasion, we had arrived too late and it was all about speed—could I have run faster from the shop, moved my kit over quicker, taken more risks behind the wheel. For the lads that had been there, their self-persecution would have had several other layers. We waited in this way for several minutes until the police gave the go ahead for the body to be released.

As I set the airbags up around the contorted corpse of a middle-aged man, I could hear the screams of a child. The police were holding back family and friends who had arrived on scene. Throughout the incident ground, eyes were scrunched shut as the wider implications of death became painfully vivid. I returned to the task at hand. Professionally and respectfully, the man was placed in a body bag. Our equipment was made up and we left the scene.

Back at the station, we moved our kit back onto the fire engine and returned to the shop to complete our inspection.

Our day continued and the incident was never mentioned again. The lack of discussion simply suggested that we had all reached the same conclusion—there was nothing we could have done. Nevertheless, the images and sounds of the incident would remain with me, and I doubt I was alone in hugging my child a little tighter that night.

On that occasion, I don't believe we could have saved that man's life. Paramedics had testified to the fact at the scene. However, it was incontrovertible that every cut to the fire service was being felt more deeply and there was a growing sense of anger amongst firefighters. The crews at that motorcycle incident had exhausted all viable options as they waited for the necessary equipment to arrive. However, they repeatedly tried adapting the use of various pieces of equipment in an attempt to save a life. Their desperation increased with every passing second. They could have predicted from the outset they would fail. However, trying was infinitely better than standing idly by, watching someone die.

I saw the two periods of industrial action and the opposition to brutal cuts in a similar vein. We had to try, but ultimately it was always out of our hands. Statistics had been modified to provide justification and fire deaths became virtually impossible. However, as firefighter posts and fire engines continue to be reduced, additional resources will take longer to arrive. Consequently, the risk to both the public and firefighters inevitably increases.

Since becoming a parent, I have a greater sense of my own mortality. Incidents rarely allow for a conscious thought, but the aftermath can hit harder. Firefighting is an occupational hazard, but I have seen death in the unlikeliest places.

As dawn broke over a bank holiday, we were called to a road traffic collision. The streets were deserted, but a vehicle that had lost control struck six people waiting at a bus stop. It was a sobering reminder of the fragility of life and it is not something I take for granted.

Sadly, there has been a recent rise in firefighter fatalities, but the risk has always been there. It is ingrained in the job description, leaving none of us immune, and out of respect to our brave colleagues who have made the ultimate sacrifice, we will continually do whatever we can.

However, the pension debacle had left a bitter taste. The determination and optimism that was synonymous with firefighters evaporated as we looked to a future that involved even fewer fire engines, less personnel and working to an impossible age.

The politics were out of our hands, but we had to deal with the consequences.

I was a 38-year old single parent, with very few transferable skills and the prospect of starting again in another field did not appeal. However, I could not sustain my current role into my sixties. I felt sick with despair at the horrendously cruel timing—I had devoted 15 years to an organisation that had barely tolerated me, but just as parity was coming to the fore, I had to consider a life away from the fire service.

Thirty

The ruling on our pension scheme may have initiated my need for a new career path, but there were other underlying issues also coming to the fore.

In December 2014, we were given two weeks' notice of a change to our working hours and the New Year saw the implementation of two consecutive 15-hour day shifts, running from 0900 hours through to midnight. Whilst no-one was altogether happy with the modifications, others found it tolerable and workable. For me, it was neither. Accommodating these new shifts would be costly as I could not collect Shaun at midnight, meaning I would have to pay an additional 18 hours of childcare. However, my greatest concern was that I would not see my son for 48 hours.

I had taken the decision to adopt because I felt I could offer a child a stable, loving home. I was subsequently assessed and found to be suitable given my circumstances at the time. Our current arrangement worked brilliantly, but the amendments threw everything into turmoil. Shaun had already been through so much; further change was the last thing he needed.

The fact that my family lived over two hours' drive away compounded the issue so I asked senior management for my unique circumstances to be taken into account.

This, perhaps inevitably, drew sudden, unwanted attention to my single-parent status. Maddeningly, after 15 years of fighting for equality as a female firefighter, I faced a different battle as my private life was now considered very public property.

I was fielding questions from management and I felt my parenting was being unfairly scrutinized. On one occasion, I was sitting in a lecture with the rest of my watch, when the new shift system was brought up. Billy, my crew manager, highlighted numerous issues. My own circumstances aside, several of my workmates had concerns. However, the station manager decided to address me personally:

'What do you do when you have a busy night shift and you have to go home and look after your child?'

Billy answered eloquently on my behalf: 'Hang on a second. Kate is not the only parent in the room! Everyone who has kids is in the same boat.'

He reeled off half the lads, jabbing a finger in their direction as he explained that they would have sole responsibility for their children when they returned home. Their wives and girlfriends would be at work.

'The only difference is...'

I loved Billy, he always said exactly what was on his

mind and had no desire to ingratiate himself with senior officers. He was passionate in his beliefs and his dark brows furrowed as he delivered his opinion: '...Kate is doing it by herself.'

I was given a temporary reprieve and special recompense to continue on the same shift pattern. A few months of avoidance and skirting around the issue followed. I knew the powers that be were reluctant to make it permanent, as it would have led to a barrage of similar requests. However, when I eventually met with them face to face, I was confident that an agreement could be reached. After dissecting my personal situation, I was crushed when management delivered their 'solution':

'You should take your son to your sister's house as she's married. It's very important for children to have two role models, so that will be better for him. You can drive down and drop him off in time to get back to work. Then set straight off after your last shift so you can be there for him waking up.'

Problem solved.

The brigade might have deemed it better for Shaun to stay with his aunt and uncle while I added a four-hour commute to my 15-hour working day, but I found it repugnant that someone who had never met my son could tell me with such confidence what was best for him.

"The only other alternative," I was told, "is that you transfer to a permanent role in Prevention and Education."

I felt infuriated yet vulnerable. I had support from the

lads, but the battle was unique to me and I did not want to give the brigade reason to question the robustness of my current childcare arrangements. As soon as it was suggested that I return to the office, I was wary of providing ammunition. The slightest slip—the very first time Shaun affected my working life—I felt an order was likely to be issued. I had the familiar, unpleasant sensation of living on a knife edge.

The decision on my son's childcare collided with the government's ruling on our pension scheme. My position as a firefighter now appeared untenable. I was furious and frustrated, but impotent. I had dedicated my entire working life to the fire service and now my future was hopelessly uncertain.

I needed a fall-back strategy and I craved an environment of development and infinite possibilities. I was tired of fighting an established regime and wanted to have complete autonomy over my own destiny and find my true potential. Consequently, I worked towards my personal training qualification which would allow me to set up my own business.

At the same time, I set another significant chain of events in motion as I considered adopting another child.

Shaun was brilliantly funny and fantastic company. He had an abundance of energy and positivity and his enthusiasm was infectious—life with my son was effortlessly enjoyable. I felt like a blackjack player who had drawn two kings: every sensible thought told me to stick and play the amazing hand I had been given.

I had already achieved so much and I recognised that I

had been extremely lucky so far, but ultimately I didn't want Shaun to be an only child. He was sociable and loved interaction with other children. I had a wonderful relationship with both my brothers and sister and I wanted Shaun to enjoy the delights, comfort and strength of a sibling bond. Furthermore, I recognised that I could not truly understand what it felt like to be adopted. I loved the idea of Shaun and his sibling having each other—as a mutual support, a confidante and a best friend.

"Would you say it was easier or harder having two children?"

I was sitting in the back cab, returning from a house fire in the dead of night. The smell of smoke permeated throughout the truck. I was wet, filthy and tired. In years gone by, my mind would have been on a shower, a hot cup of tea and my bed, but now I was voicing the thought that occupied my every waking moment.

There was an almost imperceptible pause as the lads digested my question, but they replied without judgement.

"It's great. Mine get on brilliantly and entertain each other so it's actually easier having two."

I nodded enthusiastically at my BA partner. It was the answer I wanted.

"You're kidding, aren't you? It's ten times harder with two!" the driver shouted back.

Billy had the deciding vote. He answered after consideration and delivered his viewpoint with typical bluntness.

"It might be easier or it might be harder. But… you have

to assume it is going to be a lot harder and consider if you still want to go ahead with it."

He was right. That was the gamble. I had to decide if I was prepared to jeopardise everything that I had worked so hard for—Shaun's happiness and stability—for the chance of a sibling bond.

The ramifications of a second child would be far reaching. From a practical point of view, I would have to postpone the start of my personal training career and I would be paying two lots of childcare that already doubled my mortgage repayments. Furthermore, I still didn't have a workable solution to the extended shifts.

Time was running out, and a permanent move to Prevention and Education department beckoned, when Ray called me into his office:

"We want to keep you, Kate. I don't want you to leave and neither do the lads."

Ray had already exceeded the greatest compliment anyone in the fire service had paid to me, but there was more: he, along with the rest of the lads, offered to cover my extended days.

I could have hugged him. No-one liked the extended shifts so the offer was beyond generous, but it was the fact that Ray was actively trying to keep me on the watch that meant the world to me.

I sat for a while, swallowing hard to dislodge the lump that was forming in my throat, before delivering my verdict.

"Ray, that is the kindest, most thoughtful thing anyone

has ever done for me, but I can't accept."

My big-hearted watch manager looked bewildered. "Why not?"

"Because I don't want my choices and my life to have a negative impact on you and the lads. It's not fair."

"Yes, but we wouldn't have offered if we didn't mean it. Even if we just did it for a year, it would tide you over until Shaun started school and then it would make things easier for you."

It was a wonderful gesture, but I wanted to be in control of my life, not beholden to others. It was unfair to ask the lads to help me out while I was considering adopting a second child.

Ray understood and I overheard him relaying our conversation to my station manager, who made his opinion perfectly clear.

"A second child? What the fuck is she thinking? How can she afford that?"

To a degree, I could see his point of view—my childcare arrangements were already highlighted as inadequate. However, from my perspective, the problem was not going to go away and the number of children I had was largely irrelevant. My watch agreed:

"I didn't have to get the brigade's permission when wor lass got pregnant!" one of the lads laughed. "Whether you choose to have children or not, it's none of their business!"

"How does he know how much money you have?" Billy asked. "Besides, it's not like you can accidentally adopt a child!"

They were right and incredibly supportive. Their offer to work my extended shifts spoke volumes of their characters and cemented my belief that the fire service was changing. I was angry at certain individuals, but the masses no longer sat back and allowed them to get away with it. Harassment, intolerance and bullying behaviour was challenged at the source, a new era beckoned, but it was still frustratingly out of my reach.

I focused on the elements of my life that were in my control and after discussing the implications at length with Shaun and the rest of my family, I applied to adopt a second child.

Although my current prospects in the fire service were miserably limited, I still had a job and with it, relative financial security. From a practical point of view, my adoption application would look more favourable whilst I was in steady employment rather than starting out as a new business. I also had the adoption leave to consider. In terms of my personal desires, I wanted a younger child to preserve Shaun's status as the eldest, and I wanted my children to be close in age. The timing may not have been ideal, but I felt it was right.

The process was quicker the second-time around as much of the groundwork had already been completed—I applied in April 2015 and had my medical the following month.

Adoption medicals are far more comprehensive than

any assessment I have undergone in the fire service. In a 90-minute period, I was poked and prodded, tested for every conceivable disease and abnormality to eliminate any concern that a placed child may be subjected to more grief and loss. It was during this test that a weakness was discovered in my left hand. In truth, I had been aware—shooting pains travelled up my arm every time I grabbed a weight, but practically every firefighter carried some form of injury. I was able to work around it and assumed the problem would rectify itself in time. My doctor did not appear overly concerned, but I was sent for further tests. A trapped nerve was mooted as the most plausible cause, which could be easily rectified.

I had to return to the prevention and education office when my doctor highlighted the problem. At first, I thought it would be a quick fix, but appointments were hard to come by and the saga dragged on. I missed the lads and the job, but I always felt like my return was tangibly close. My family had all offered to have Shaun for my extended days and I had decided that when the time came, I could see how he would cope.

In the meantime, my second adoption application progressed and I was approved at the panel hearing on July 3rd, 2015—two years, almost to the day, since I first learned of Shaun.

Two months later, on September 25th, I was handed a file containing the particulars of a little boy.

My prior experience meant I was better prepared.

However, the matching process was far more difficult as I had Shaun to consider—I had to make sure the match was right for everyone. I read the notes with a detached outlook and tried not to get drawn in, but I couldn't help it. The little guy sounded perfect, but there was a vast number of unknowns. There were concerns surrounding his ability to hear, talk and walk. Even at 18 months old—an age with very few certainties regarding development, he had more questions than most.

Hoping for the best is a mindset I live by, but when my actions affect other people, guilt and self-doubt reign. Shaun was my main consideration and I was not prepared for the challenges that may arise with a child with significant additional needs. However, there was an equal chance that in the right environment, the boy would flourish and meet all his expected milestones. It was an impossible decision.

I kept it all from Shaun and decided to request additional information. I would hear from every significant person involved in the toddler's life, from foster carers and social workers to health visitors and medical advisors. The picture would be clearer, but with every new discovery, I would be drawn deeper into his world, making it harder to walk away.

Throughout that whole period of time I was undergoing further tests on my hand. There were no guarantees, but the odds were firmly in my favour. Equally, I imagined the toddler awaiting assessments, but his carers having a certain expectation of the outcome. Consequently, I went into the meeting with an open mind and listened intently to what the professionals had to say.

They described a gorgeous little boy who was developing at a rate that fit with his background. He was settled and happy in his foster placement, and with abundant love and support he was making progress with his walking and communication skills. Some of the care workers broke down as they described his warm, placid and playful personality. As they spoke, I imagined the two boys together and made up my mind.

In November 2015, Thomas and I were approved at the matching panel.

I excitedly returned home and began preparing Shaun for the imminent arrival of his little brother.

Shaun had been asking for a brother from the moment he could talk and was past himself in excitement, announcing to everyone, "Mummy is getting me a brother for Christmas!"

Strangers would shoot me a look that thankfully suggested I did not look 8 months pregnant. I would smile in agreement with my son, making us both appear entirely bonkers. However, as things turned out, Thomas did not come home for Christmas.

There was a delay in the courts and Thomas's hearing was postponed on three separate occasions. Melanie rang me at home during the first week in December.

"We can't get Thomas' case heard in time for Christmas."

It was infuriating, but it was out of my hands. It was

Shaun I felt sorry for. I had built up his expectations and now I had to explain to a four-year-old that there had been a change of plan.

Once again, Shaun astounded me with his ability to just roll with things and we enjoyed a final Christmas as a twosome. Thomas, however, was never far from my thoughts—I couldn't wait until my two boys were together.

Thomas' case was finally heard at the end of January, and only took 15 minutes of the courts schedule.

On Monday, 8th February, 2016, I dropped Shaun at nursery and met Thomas for the first time. He was a beautiful little boy with blonde hair and gorgeous brown eyes. He clung to Jill, his foster carer, but soon took some tentative steps towards me and my heart melted as he flashed me a smile.

For the next few days, I gradually built up the time I was spending with Thomas, but I was having to leave one child to see the other and I constantly felt torn, a part of me was always missing.

On Thursday, I woke early, giddy with anticipation. It was the day my boys would meet for the first time.

I was excited, but nervous. My heart raced as my eyes kept flitting to the clock at Jill's house. Ben and his wife were bringing Shaun over at 2pm and from half past one I felt sick. I tried to concentrate on what Jill was saying, but my head was swimming. My stomach felt empty yet I could not eat anything. Finally, there was a knock on the door.

Jill answered it as I watched Thomas. I could hear

Shaun shout: "Is my brother here?" My heart burst and I was choking back tears. I needed to be with Shaun and switched places with Jill. I squeezed him tight as I thanked my friends. They made a swift exit and I had a second alone with Shaun in the hallway.

"Are you ok?"

"Yes, can I see my brother now?"

"Of course you can. He's just through there."

Shaun walked with purpose to the kitchen door. He turned for a second, smiling at me, his eyes dancing with delight, inviting me to share in his excitement and seeking permission.

I nodded.

Shaun pushed the door open and even from behind, I could see his cheeks stretch into a huge smile, reflected in Thomas' face. Both boys stood a foot away from each other, staring into each other's eyes, with a fixed, open mouthed grin.

I sat down. "Are you going to say hi?"

"Hi," Shaun shot up a hand, almost in a trance.

Thomas was fascinated and gingerly reached up. As Shaun moved to meet him, their hands touched for the first time. The connection was both instant and electric. The boys shrieked with delight, before collapsing in giggles.

It was a moment that I will never forget.

Thirty-One

On Sunday, Valentine's Day, Shaun and I collected Thomas to begin our new lives together. As I drove home, cherishing the sound of the boys' laughter, I could not imagine being happier.

"Mum. Mum!" Shaun's cry sounded urgent. I parked up and turned around expecting him to need the toilet. Instead he just smiled and pointed to his brother.

"Where did we get this boy from again?!"

I looked at Thomas who was grinning manically at me.

"We got your brother from his foster carer didn't we."

"Yes, that's right, and we don't have to take him back, do we?"

"No, darling."

"Did you hear that, Thomas! You can stay with us forever and you will always be my brother."

Thomas nodded happily at the excitement in Shaun's voice.

I knew Shaun struggled. That despite his raucous exterior, he was a timid, sensitive soul who hated goodbyes because in his experience they were forever. I knew he was terrified of failing because he thought that equated to not being good enough to stay with the people he loved. And I knew that large sections of society did not see that. Strangers would comment if his temper flared or if he lashed out. Loud tuts and declarations of 'what that child needs' upset and angered me. There were many times when I wanted to scream at someone and educate them, but increasingly I was at peace with my world. I had learned to disregard the opinions of people that did not matter to me and as I looked at my sons' contented faces, I was thankful beyond words that they would always have each other.

My second period of adoption leave got off to a difficult start as I was flawed with a chest infection. I spent a large amount of time prone on the couch as the boys played. I accepted help when I could—friends took Shaun to nursery twice a week and to his swimming lesson, but I could not let them help with Thomas, as he needed time to settle and attach with me. It was a tough three weeks before my GP was able to prescribe antibiotics.

My boys were incredible. They had both been single children, enjoying the complete attention of their primary carer, and yet with very little guidance, they carved out a beautiful brotherly bond. I marvelled at their ability to take such upheaval in their stride and I loved observing their playfulness as they explored their relationship.

As soon as I felt better, I took Shaun and Thomas on a much-needed outing to soft play. I met with Jen and enjoyed some adult conversation while the boys played.

It was blissful and liberating. I felt that we could finally start enjoying this exciting new chapter of our lives. I savoured the simple delights of a drink with a friend, soaking up the aroma of the coffee beans along with Jen's news. Amongst the excited screams of playful children, I enjoyed a wonderful sense of serenity. Turbulent times had a habit of making me appreciate everyday moments.

Jen and I said our goodbyes on the pavement as Shaun climbed obligingly into his car seat. Thomas was mid tantrum, devastated to leave the soft play, but I was not prepared to reason with him while I was exposed on the road side. Fortunately, his slight frame was easily manhandled into his seat.

I had the final strap in my hands when I heard the gut-wrenching screeching of brakes. Thomas' screams stopped in an instant and Shaun cried "MUM!" a split second before I felt the impact of a car on my left side, throwing me against the open door. The sickening sound of metal on metal followed as my car door was ripped from its hinges.

Miraculously, I held Thomas in place and secured the clasp. Both boys were white with shock.

"Are you ok?" I smiled reassuringly at them.

They nodded, their little mouths opened wide and their eyes fixed on me.

"I saw everything!" Jen was breathless as she joined me. "How are you still standing?"

I surveyed the carnage—broken glass littered the road,

the front of my car had crumpled from the impact and the door was hanging limply by wires.

It did not make sense.

I was light headed and disoriented, but managed to phone Ben while Jen reported the accident. I reluctantly relinquished the boys to Ben's wife—I worried it was too soon for Thomas, but my friends and the paramedics persuaded me to get checked out.

The oncoming car had hit me on my left side, an inch from my hip. My right-hand side had struck the open door and both my shins had hit the underside of my car. I was sore, but extremely lucky and returned home with a diagnosis of extensive bruising and whiplash.

I cannot deny that the accident affected me. I was jumpy walking along a road and more considered behind a wheel. I no longer trusted other drivers' actions on the road. It also made me rethink the direction my life was going—I didn't want to leave this world with regrets and vowed to treasure every moment, seize every opportunity and prioritise time with my two amazing boys.

It was not just the collision—my second period of adoption leave was far more enjoyable. The boys were brilliant company, I had adjusted to motherhood and I had learned from my many previous mistakes. I loved every minute of being off. In contrast, every dealing I had with the fire service throughout my leave left a bitter taste.

My hand was not improving, so I was regularly summoned to visit the brigade doctor. The boys now attended nursery for one day a week, allowing me some much needed 'Kate time'. Taking two hours out of that day to update occupational health was costly and irksome. I was already annoyed when I sat down for the consultation.

"So…" The middle-aged doctor with a suit, tie and sweeping fringe picked up my file. "The problem is with your left hand. What is wrong with it?"

I inhaled deeply, frustrated at revisiting old ground. "I don't have any strength in it and now I'm worried that the muscles are wasting and I won't get them back."

"I see," he nods at my dossier. "Maybe it's because you're right handed?"

I looked at him with bewildered contempt.

"I'm a firefighter," I explained to the top of his head. "I have always wanted to be a firefighter and I love being a firefighter. I spent 15 years operational, but I had to come off the trucks because I have no grip in my left hand."

I paused, wondering if that was enough, however his confused expression encouraged me to continue.

"I need to be able to lift ladders, climb ladders, hold equipment, cut people out of cars, carry people out of fires. All of those require me to use two hands. So why would being right handed suddenly cause my left hand to go weak?"

The doctor didn't answer, but was reading my file intently. I wasn't prepared for his next question.

"What does your partner do?"

"I don't have one."

"But you have two children."

"I adopted them."

"Why? You could have just fostered them."

"I didn't want to foster them, I wanted to adopt them."

"Who is looking after the children now?"

"They're at nursery."

"What is their background?"

I stopped. His entire line of questioning was inappropriate. He had caught me off guard and I was incensed. My heart rate soared and I felt a well of anger bubbling in the pit of my stomach.

"That is none of your business. My children's backgrounds belong to them. If they want to tell anyone they can, it's not my place."

"Well, I think they would be better off if you stayed in the department. You don't want to go back as a firefighter."

I was livid, but determined not to show a reaction. Holding his stare, I declared,

"That is interesting, because I think it is none of your business. I am here about my hand, not to discuss my children."

I stood up and concluded.

"I will let my consultant know your diagnosis: that I am right handed."

Far from feeling supported by the brigade, my visit to the doctor left me feeling forced into a corner. A full recovery was still considered the most likely outcome, but now the doctor was seemingly supporting senior management's view that I should remain in the office. My options were becoming increasingly limited and with two boys, I had to carefully consider my future.

As 2016 drew to a close, I had exhausted all my adoption leave. Shaun was now settled at school and Thomas was thriving at nursery. We had a brilliant first Christmas as a family and I loved being able to see both of their nativity plays, soaking up every aspect of the festive season from the Polar Express to Pantomimes. In the back of my mind I was thinking, 'If I returned to shifts, I would miss all of this.'

I visited the station on Christmas Eve as my watch were on duty. The significance was not lost on me. I could not imagine not being home in the morning when my boys woke up. These are the sacrifices firefighters make—missing countless family occasions and children's milestones. Hundreds compete for handfuls of leave and colleagues will come in at four in the morning to allow parents to get home in time, but demand far outweighs availability and the vast majority of firefighters will miss out.

I had worked at least a portion of every Christmas for the first 14 years of my career. There were times when I could not see my family at all and colleagues kindly invited me to stay with them. There were other times when I would drive down for a priceless couple of hours at my parents' house for dinner. Surrounded by the love and warmth of my family, declining alcohol as they became increasingly merry, I would leave with a heavy, aching heart for a 15-hour night shift.

I had been lucky since I had Shaun—adoption leave

and a well-timed leave entitlement meant I was able to share every Christmas with him, but I knew that would change.

Did I really want to go back? I had to be honest with myself and, taking everything into account, the answer was 'No'.

I was tired of fighting. I didn't want to work for an organisation which had consistently placed me in a box. At first as a female, now as a single parent. I increasingly felt as if their outdated opinions were placing a ceiling on my hopes and aspirations. I had turned 40 and I believed there was still time to be successful in another field, but time was ticking.

I didn't see my single parent status as a weakness, but as a strength. It showed I possessed resilience, courage and fortitude. I knew that I had grown as a person and I felt I had a lot to offer. Yet, I also realised that I was limited by the beliefs of those in power. I had the benefit of experience and the corollary to the antiquated minority who balked at my single parent status had been the sexist bigots who found it easier to find fault than admit that they were wrong. I wanted to get off the treadmill.

However, a condition of my adoption payments stipulated that I had to return to work for a minimum of 12 weeks. So, I went back in January 2017 with the intention of leaving at the end of March.

Thirty-Two

My colleagues argued I would not find a job as good as this one, and they had a point. I realised it was a gamble, but I trusted myself. I had consistently proved people wrong and I was confident that I could make my personal trainer business work.

The only stumbling block was my hand. A shoulder operation was now proposed to relieve a possible trapped nerve and I was sent for an MRI and further nerve conduction tests. As March approached, I reconciled with the fact I would have to delay my plans for a few months to allow my shoulder to recover, but when I met with the consultant my world came crashing down.

He called it Multi-Focal Neuropathy—a lifelong condition that required regular visits to the hospital on a monthly, if not weekly, basis. I would not get better, but the treatment had proved incredibly effective in halting the body's decline. My whole world was spinning out of control. I couldn't focus and pored through Google for answers. I didn't like what I found.

It took nearly a month before I could start the treatment—intravenous immunoglobulin, which would see the medication applied directly to my veins.

During that time, I became depressed and withdrawn. The thought of not being able to look after my boys terrified me and I worried endlessly. I could not see a way back to the fire engines and the idea of starting my own business with two young children around a comprehensive hospital schedule appeared impossible. I therefore applied for a permanent post in prevention and education. I had to be grateful for what I had and I needed to protect my financial future.

I had two full days of treatment, surrounded by people who were going through the same thing. One woman told me she had been coming weekly for 18 years. She explained that she chose to receive treatment on Friday, in case she reacted badly: she then had three good days where she was able to look after her grandchildren. My hand symptoms were similar, but others didn't fit.

"Everyone is different," she explained, "which is what makes it so difficult to diagnose. But, you must have noticed that you were tired all the time?"

I laughed. "I'm a single parent with two little boys. I expect to be tired all the time!"

I was in awe of everyone I met during those two days and buoyed by their inspirational stories. One young man ran his business while he was attached to a drip. Another told me that most of his family and friends didn't even know he was ill. I couldn't be down in their company and I resolved to ensure I made the most of the time I was well.

I reacted badly to the treatment and endured excruciating headaches alongside three days of constant nausea, unable to keep water down. I hated the effect my infirmity had on my boys and dreaded my next infusion.

Ben had recently retired and I was working alone. I visited vulnerable people; a young mother who bravely sat and described the prognosis of her degenerative disease as her children played and her husband planned the necessary renovations and fire safety precautions, elderly people who had just lost their life-long partner and hoarders whose lives were confined to a single metre squared.

I found it intensely challenging. As a firefighter you walk away and leave the occupants to deal with the aftermath of a fire or road traffic collision, but now I was finding it increasingly difficult to switch off. I saw hope rise in desolate eyes as they rested on my uniform and warmth radiate from broken hearts as they welcomed me into their home. I don't know if my presence was a welcome distraction or an opportunity to offload, but they trusted me by virtue of my employment and that spoke volumes of our work.

It was a privilege, but it was also consuming and draining. I was struggling to come to terms with my recent diagnosis, maintain an empathetic ear throughout the day and a positive demeanour in front of the boys. I was running on empty.

I returned to the station every lunchtime. It was an

opportunity to go to the gym and offload to the rest of my team. I was washing cups when I bumped into an embittered crew manager. He nodded at the cups as he sneered,

"I bet that's the most work you've done today."

There was a widespread assumption that the people who worked in my department had it easy. I glanced at him as he folded his washing and smiled. He was a regular grumbler, widely assuming that everyone else had a smoother ride and that life owed him a living. It seemed to leave him almost perpetually miserable and in that very moment, I realised how lucky I was.

I had witnessed enough of life to understand that I was advantaged from birth. I had faced enough obstacles to know that each one was surmountable and I have never felt the need to put anyone down. I suddenly realised that the issues some people had with my gender or single parent status said far more about them than of me. If you consistently seek fault elsewhere, your circumstances are unlikely to improve.

Multifocal neuropathy terrified me, but facing it head on allayed many of my fears. I spoke to the experts—people who had lived with the condition for years. I also spoke with their family members to find out the wider repercussions. I discovered the best way to limit the horrendous side effects and clung to the fact that some people can manage on monthly infusions.

When I returned to see the consultant, the treatment showed a significant health improvement. However, this was not accompanied with the expected subsequent decline. It indicated either a misdiagnosis or potentially a substantial period between infusions. I was elated and left the hospital feeling ten feet tall.

The whole experience had been horrific, but was yet another reminder that life was for living.

On my triumphant return to work, fresh from my consultation and high on life, an advert caught my attention— instructors were being enlisted for the Training School. There had been an 8-year freeze in firefighter recruitment and the role of the current instructors was focused on the delivery of training to operational crews. A restructure had reduced their rank and subsequent pay, but it was still an extremely attractive position for me. It would allow me to remain on a flexible day time shift pattern and it would provide a brilliant opportunity to develop my skills and have a more active and physical role. Furthermore, I had enjoyed training the young firefighters and new recruits posted to my watch. I had the experience, the skill set and the qualifications required.

"I'm going to apply!" I declared to the lads in the office.

They laughed.

"Good luck with that one!" said Micky—an openly gay guy. He professed to being two years younger than me, but suffered every ailment known to man and had an opinion on everything. "You have no chance of getting it!"

"I might." I was determined, but tentative—doubt was setting in.

"If you get that job, I will show my arse in Fenwicks' window!"

Mooning in a department shop would be highly irregular, but equally, in seventeen years, I had only seen one female firefighter get promoted. I could see his point.

As I remained silent, contemplating my next move, my colleague laid all the facts bare.

"Seriously, Kate," Micky was on a roll, "you are a woman, a single parent and you are gay. Therefore, you are literally the last person they would give a promotion to!"

I rolled my eyes. "I told you, I'm not gay, but…I see your point."

By now Micky was in hysterics at my ludicrous idea to better myself.

"Bloody hell, Kate, you're even behind me! I might be as queer as Christmas but at least I'm a guy!"

The conversation continued without me. Arms folded, I was staring into space, completely immersed in my own thoughts.

Unfortunately, everything Micky had said was true.

The promotion process was widely regarded as a joke, as personality factors are supposedly taken into account.

Considerate bosses have devised this system to ensure that 'round pegs are not put in square holes'. Each watch is unique and certain characters may be better suited to some than others. This is understandable, as is utilising an individual's knowledge and experience on specialist equipment and harnessing it to a particular station.

However, it leaves the scheme vulnerable to manipulation for personal gain. This lack of clarity has caused many potential managers to lose confidence in the promotion system.

From my perspective, I've found it a farce.

There were 72 watches in the brigade when I received my first posting. Although I had selected three preferred stations, I understood that I could have been sent anywhere. Yet, I was placed on a watch with a station officer who was very candid about his feelings towards female firefighters. Simon's intentions were also well known. The system is designed for adjustments, but it's very apparent whom they favour.

Nevertheless, the brigade was undoubtedly changing as a new Chief had recently been instated. He had risen through the ranks with impressive purpose and his success at the final hurdle was met with a mixture of surprise and delight. He was atypical of senior management by virtue of his accessibility. He was relatable and approachable. He appeared to retain the heart and ideals of a firefighter and his appointment spread hope throughout the workforce.

Furthermore, I considered the role of Instructor as ideal for my circumstances and therefore felt compelled to try. Ultimately, it was my last roll of the dice. Failure would cement my decision to leave.

I was offered an interview and the subsequent feedback suggested that it had gone well. I was buoyed, positive and optimistic—enjoying the sense that change was in the air.

Even Micky had changed his tune.

"Well, to be fair, they do need a woman at the training school…it looks good!"

Yet days went by and I didn't hear anything. Then weeks passed and the brigade gossip lines delivered the news—all the available posts had been filled.

I continued to work with the prevention team, but I found the lone working, coupled with the intense nature of my visits, extremely hard. I loved delivering sessions to schools. However, I struggled to sit through photo albums of recently departed loved ones and provide comfort when it was needed. I was there to deliver fire safety information and fit smoke alarms, but I was a visitor in their home and it could take several minutes to steer the conversation. I felt trapped in the department and it was not where I wanted to be.

During the summer of 2017, a two week break in Scotland cemented my decision to leave the fire service. It was only by removing myself from work that I realised I was spent, physically and emotionally. My boys were my world and I didn't want stress to seep into our family life. They would experience more upheaval as they adjusted to a new school year in September so I decided to request reduced hours to ensure that I was more readily available to help them.

My application to work part time landed at the desk of Claire, a Station Manager. My brigade did have ranking female officers. These women were from the corporate side of the business and had never been firefighters. Perversely, the fact they had no firefighting experience limited their career prospects almost as much as being a firefighter had limited mine. The rank was misleading as Claire didn't have a station to manage, but she led the Prevention team and headed up the Gender Group.

She arranged to meet with me in person and fully supported my decision and right to reduce my hours. Moreover, Claire's rank meant that her view of the entire organisation was far superior to mine.

My perspective was limited to my immediate environment. Therefore, I took the views of my station manager and the brigade doctor to be representative of the brigade. However, Claire assured me that the upper echelons of the brigade were conscientiously working towards diversity and inclusion. Pushing tirelessly for equality and flexibility, Claire was passionate that a firefighter's personal circumstances should not hinder their advancement. Her efficiency, encouragement and candour impressed me and for the first time, I found myself speaking to someone who actually understood my frustrations.

Claire invited me to a Gender Conference, to be hosted by our fire service the following month. "Come along and see how you find it."

I had nothing to lose and there was talk of a decent buffet.

I didn't arrive with an open mind. I had already decided it would be a showcase of false promises. An opportunity for high-ranking officers to wallow in self-praise as they regaled accounts of a glorified inclusive workforce.

I was way off beam.

The conference room was filled to capacity with employees from every rank and department. The whole day was orchestrated to promote excellence in gender equality, highlighting that although the UK had introduced both the Equality Pay Act and the Sex Discrimination Act before I was born, gender inequality had not gone away.

Our new Chief had the room with his opening statement "I know that I am privileged as a white, male, heterosexual…I know it has helped me get to where I am today…"

Finally.

Thirty-Three

It was not the fact he recognised he was privileged, nor the fact he could ascertain that those three traits helped. It was the fact he could acknowledge the labels did not define him. It is one of the great paradoxes of modern society that we can identify as anything we want: queer, agender, cisgender, non-binary, to name a few, yet we struggle to properly identify with ourselves.

Despite the fact I don't like labels, I now recognise that they are an inescapable part of life as people, consciously or not, assign others into categories. I may have consistently tried to distance myself from the assumptions linked to certain groups, but there is one label I have never hidden from—I am a mum. I am immensely proud of my children and being their parent means the world to me. Nevertheless, I am struck by the disparities associated with working parents. Dads are seen as hardworking, focussed and career driven. They are loyal employees worthy of investment through development and promotion. Working mums, however, are viewed with suspicion from employers and colleagues as someone who would ditch work the second their kids needed them. It is completely unfair to both sides—I have seen many dads leave work at a moment's notice because having priorities in order is linked to the individual and not the gender. Equally, leaving work early once or twice a year to collect a poorly child does not detract from one's commitment to their career.

My biggest issue with labelling is that it is lazy, judgemental and stagnant. It is a snapshot that favours the privileged, but it would not be an issue if people could see beyond the obvious and unveil the whole person. The sub groups by which we are categorised have been around for generations yet our understanding of the people within has not morphed with time. We are all complex individuals, with unique histories, needs and desires, and we deserve to be treated as such. I sport many labels, but not one of them has defined who I am.

I don't believe it is possible to fully relate to others without understanding yourself. I am white, female and I am a Firefighter. There is no requirement for a prefix, just as doctors, teachers, astronauts, footballers, scientists and any other profession the world over are not described by their gender. I am also a parent who happens to be single and work.

Whilst I have never understood the furore surrounding sexuality, I appreciate that my ignorance equates to privilege. I do not define myself by my choice of partner but I have never felt the need to hide any aspect of my life. While

I worked as a gym instructor at Newcastle University, I was threatened by an older member of staff. If I didn't do as she had asked, she would tell everyone that I was gay.

I laughed. "Go ahead," I told her. "I could not care less."

I knew she didn't understand. She was in her late forties and was terrified that people would discover that she herself had a girlfriend. It was a fear that consumed far too many people when they talk about 'coming out'. Furthermore, the terror and distress materialised from extremely valid consequences. Some young teenagers are forcibly ejected from their family home and disowned by their loved ones, homophobic attacks remain a regular occurrence and being gay is still tossed into the mix of supposed good natured insults.

Sexuality may have been immaterial to me, but Adam had not stopped at white and male when he described the ideal firefighter, heterosexuality was also considered a key ingredient. Ignorance can not be fought with silence, yet the fight for equality from the LGBT community has an added layer of difficulty. Gender and colour are easily identifiable, whereas the mask of invisibility cloaked over sexuality has to be forcibly removed before progress can be made. It requires courage from each individual to stand up and commit for the action cannot be reversed. The responsibility should be shared by the workforce, the organisation and the community by creating a welcoming, tolerant environment and terminating the jibes, abuse and prejudice.

I am lucky that my sexuality has never defined me, but I have never hidden from who I am. I am pansexual. I love someone for who they are, not because of their gender.

I am a mum, a daughter, a sister, a sister-in law, an auntie, a cousin, a friend and a colleague. I am the product of every interaction and experience, positive or not, that have forged me into the person I am today.

I have heard many people say that they don't see colour, nor gender, just the person. However, in 17 years as a fire-fighter, no-one saw me.

Nobody noticed that I was crushed when I discovered Adam's views on the ideal firefighter. Nobody noted that I repeatedly requested development beyond my current role. Nobody saw that I was treated differently from the rest of my watch and nobody questioned why I wanted to leave. Turning a convenient blind eye is not the answer. Perhaps, it is time we opened our eyes.

The fact our new Chief was able to categorise himself told me he could see.

He was white, male and heterosexual, but he was also a leader with incredible emotional intelligence. He concluded his opening speech by acknowledging the responsibility that accompanies privilege. If only more people shared the incli-nation to level the playing field.

I didn't want to classify myself as a minority member. My gender and parental status are not the core definition of who I am. However, they are indisputably a part of me. I didn't want a prefix, but by fitting in I had inadvertently contributed to the lack of progress for female firefighters. I had been one of the lads, nestled on the inside, assured of acceptance as long as I didn't upset the status quo. That is not acceptance, that is a tenuous, conditional tolerance.

The geography of the service made it difficult to speak with the other lasses. We were all isolated on separate stations and different watches. Occasionally we would be detached and see someone fleetingly at a change of shift, but we were individually tasked to deal with our own problems. We had each stood alone in a male dominated domain, faced our own battles and endured intense scrutiny from various managers and officers who had wanted us to fail. Yet, we had stood our ground, proved ourselves hundreds of times over, and in doing so carved out a good reputation amongst our own watches. I had been the subject of fabricated stories and I realised the bulk of what I heard over the brigade grapevine regarding female firefighters was also likely to have been concocted over a mess table. They all have my total respect.

The Chief had set the tone and the conference room buzzed with genuine interest and fervour as the guest speakers each took to the stage.

When we stopped for a mid-morning break, two senior managers asked to speak to me. They had heard of my request for flexible working and wanted to make sure I was aware that was also an option if I wanted to return to the operational side. There had been no suggestion of that when I had an issue with the extended day shift, but it would provide a perfect balance. As I settled back into my seat, I felt at peace. My world had opened up and for the first time in a long time, I felt included, involved and valued.

I was buoyed by the day's events and the feeling of momentum. My move back to the operational side stalled slightly as good intentions met practical difficulties, but I arranged a medical to minimise any necessary delays.

I was concerned about the weakness in my left hand, but I passed the same grip test I had 20 years earlier along with the other assessments which deemed me to be fit for operational duties. I was just completing the vision examination when the nurse exclaimed,

"Have you seen they've opened up recruitment? My daughter wants to apply, what do you think?"

Her cheerful words hit me like a blow to the stomach. I froze for a beat before composing myself and forcing a smile. The nurse was lovely, bright and sociable. I imagined her daughter would be exactly the same. She continued to chat excitedly, but it was indecipherable. I was caught in a bubble of time. The past 18 years flashed in front of me and I saw my 22-year old self. My heart was racing, pounding in my chest. At this moment, with the benefit of hindsight, would I have encouraged my younger, idealistic self to join the fire service?

No. I wouldn't.

You get one chance at life. One opportunity to see how far you can take yourself. I believe in self actualisation and being all you can be. This can only be achieved by pushing yourself and encouraging others to go beyond preconceived limits and fully explore the depths of possibilities. I wanted that in a career. Instead my ability was immaterial, my appointment and any subsequent promotion attributed to the latest political agenda and my prospects miserably limited by small minded individuals and an organisation who pandered to them.

However, I also recognised that no-one would have deterred me when I first set my mind on firefighting. If I couldn't persuade females to stay away, I had to ensure their experiences were better than mine.

Thirty-Four

Twelve months have passed since I attended the Gender Conference. A position became available at the Training School and as the only remaining candidate, I was offered a temporary promotion. The fact that I was at the bottom of the list conveniently refuted claims that my gender counted in my favour.

My request for flexible hours was successful and I now work a four-day week with an incredible group of people, each of them confident in their own abilities. It is like being on a watch, yet it is unique in that every member wants to improve not only themselves, but each other. They have each experienced stepping out from the comfortable confines of a group and making a decision as an individual. Consequently, their thoughts and views are their own and there is a refreshing absence of grumbling, finger pointing and disparaging remarks.

My boys are settled and happy. They are both remarkable young people who have helped me see the world through their eyes. They love their childminder and have a steady routine. I only have to look at them to realise how lucky and privileged I am. The fact I was born into a stable, secure and happy home does not make me a more deserving mother. I have nothing but respect for Shaun and Thomas' birth Mam's. The boys have two sets of families who love them and want what is best for them.

The north east of England is a brilliant place to live and work, the people are famously friendly and I love their no nonsense, down to earth way of talking. However, I could not understand how a city that was within a three-hour train journey to London could be so far behind our famous capital. Despite having won numerous awards for equality, my brigade still lags decades behind in terms of career advancement for female firefighters. Dani Cotton's appointment as head of the London Fire Brigade illustrates the magnitude of the chasm.

Thirty-Five

To a large extent, I blamed the government targets for female firefighters. In my opinion, they created unnecessary animosity as our selection was continually questioned. Forcing brigades throughout the country to recruit women had reduced our worth. We were seen as a number, tolerated as such and placed in a pigeon hole with an expectation that we should be grateful.

I regret the time I spent appeasing sections of the fire service for my inclusion, almost apologetically tolerating their contempt. I had passed the selection criteria and was awarded a place on merit. Proving my worth to people who tenaciously repudiated my every effort was a ridiculous waste of time. I fell in with the masses, distancing myself from controversy and perceived weakness, I concealed my differences and was reluctant to upset the status quo.

However, I have realised that my sense of worth lies within. I don't need a rank or the approval of others. I've learned to trust myself, to recognise my own strengths and follow my own path. I'm motivated by a need to achieve rather than a desire to circumvent failure and I celebrate my individuality. I have been told by dozens of people that they could not do what I am doing—raising two children as a single, working parent. It highlighted huge positives to being different. Conforming to expectations had restricted my horizons, whereas my own path can take me anywhere.

I love my work life balance, my job and the feeling of genuine inclusion. The Fire Service is changing. It has taken far longer than I ever expected and we still have a long way to go, but the drive for equality is now powered by a passionate fervour rather than a stale desire to tick boxes. Attitudes and beliefs have morphed and females are ingrained amongst the firefighter contingent.

The past 20 years have been difficult, with enforced cuts, changes to pensions and working conditions, and strike action, it cannot have been an easy time to lead. Consequently, there may have been a tendency to brush individual concerns to one side and deal with the supposed bigger picture. Minority groups were further marginalised and retention figures suffered.

Nevertheless, the cuts have been ongoing and resources are still continually monitored and redeployed to maximise efficiency in order to create the safest possible community. Yet, in the same way Adam reassigned priorities at my very first flooding incident to maximise results, we needed a principal officer who saw the bigger picture. Thankfully, a united, inclusive workforce is now viewed as our single most valued commodity. As differences are noted and celebrated, we move away from a convenient collective mediocrity and maximise every individual contribution towards a common goal. For the first time, I can recommend my job to others.

Change may be positive from my perspective, but as the see saw of gender inequality begins to tip, it is met with outcry from those on the other side. The targets were seen as an affront to parity when in reality they had done little to increase female recruitment. Now women are actively encouraged to seek promotion, it is widely viewed as an unfair advantage. For over a decade I watched as firefighters were approached by senior managers who asked them to consider promotion, yet as soon as the interest is extended to females, indignation reigns and shouts of 'it's not fair' echo through the station walls.

When you are accustomed to privilege, equality can feel like oppression.

I liken the disparity to adoption. I flinch when well-meaning people comment as to how lucky my boys are. The vast majority of children are loved and cared for from birth in a stable, happy home and form strong attachments to their primary caregivers. However, when my children found their permanent home, two months before their second birthday, they are the ones considered fortunate.

I cannot dispel the myth of preferential treatment, but I can present the facts.

At the time of writing, we have a total of seven female firefighters in Tyne and Wear with a rank. Aside from a recent recruitment of an Area Manager from an external brigade, there are three substantial crew managers and two others who like me, are in a temporary position. Our BAME contingent is even more sparse. We only have two firefighters with a rank identifying as BAME and neither of them are female. It has taken me 19 years to reach this point, (exactly one rank above that which I started) Our Chief transcended every rank in the same time frame and I have seen some male counterparts achieve their first promotion before they have even finished their probation. Yet, I am considered to have been 'fast tracked' to expediently reduce the gender disparity in supervisory, middle and senior management.

That very gulf could have been reduced several years ago if the gateway to promotion had not been closed to women. We stood at the entrance for over a decade and watched as our male colleagues passed effortlessly by. It stands to reason that now the doors are open, there are several women in the queue. We account for less than 5% of operational management, yet we are the convenient excuse for any male who does not get a job.

To my male colleagues, frustrated that their opportunities have been reduced by a miniscule amount, I would say be grateful that your entire career is not belittled by a quota.

Be thankful that although we passed the same tests your selection was automatically assumed to be earned whereas mine was not. Your success was attributed to your merits rather than a protected characteristic and you were accepted from the moment you walked through the training centre doors. Be glad that you will never understand the sensation of being an imposter in the workplace, or feel the isolation of being told that you are not welcome and that you do not belong. Appreciate your line manager setting aside time to practise your probationary exams and be content that your colleagues did not refuse to work with you simply because of your gender.

My ascent of Kilimanjaro highlighted the fact that everyone's journey is unique and incomparable. Three days in, I was suffering intensely with the altitude. I couldn't eat, was violently sick and had excruciating headaches. However, by day four, I had acclimatised, and felt better. Conversely, I later discovered that those unaffected were struggling with self-doubt, completely unaware of how they would react if altitude sickness did take hold, they second guessed their abilities to cope and worried that their progress was driven by mere luck. The effects of altitude were entirely out of our hands and as each of us undertook a personal pilgrimage, we had very different experiences of virtually the same footsteps. However, the goal was universal and every person who climbed to Uhuru Peak at 5895m deserved to be there.

It was immaterial if you suffered ill effects or not, took longer than most or sprinted up, a thousand people could join you at the top and it will still take nothing away from your success.

As the sun rose over Kilimanjaro, there was no appetite for comparisons, or need to scrutinise and belittle the trek of others. It was simply a time to survey a glorious sunrise and appreciate exactly where you were.

It is too easy to blame others and circumstances for our own shortcomings. I attributed my lack of opportunity to the entire service, when in reality I failed to look beyond my immediate environment. I cannot accuse management of not listening if I am not prepared to explain. One of the many magical aspects of adopting is the knowledge that every decision I have made has led me to my two amazing boys. It shows that I am exactly where I am supposed to be. In the same vein, I appreciate every experience and setback because they have helped shape the person I am. My gender has forced me to prove myself far beyond any official probationary period. It has made me resilient, competent, resourceful and determined. So, to those people who sneer at political correctness, you are right. I have got to where I am today because I am a woman.

Acknowledgments

I am indebted to the team at Jacaranda Publishing for their help and support throughout. Particular thanks to Cherise Lopes-Baker, Laure Deprez and Vimbai Shire for their patience and guidance in transforming my ramblings into a finished product.

Thank you to my family—my incredible boys, my parents, siblings, in-laws, nephews, nieces and extended family—for your unconditional love and encouragement in everything I do.

Thanks to my friends, in particular, Pamela Dixon who inspired me to write in the first place, Jennifer Brennan, Laura Foad, Dennis O'Donnell and Beverley Walker who have all been a rock of support to myself and the boys. Thanks also to my football team mates and players who I now consider great friends, my school mates who have always stuck by me, Heidi Reynolds for her endless patience and Sophie Cherel who will never fully appreciate the extent she inspires others.

Thanks to my fire service family—colleagues who have become firm friends and enable the work life balance I enjoy today. I am grateful to Terry Griffin for his leadership, guidance and backing. 'Griff' epitomises what I believe a manager should be. Thanks also to Brian Waugh, Marcus Robinson, David Johnson, Rob Birt, Gavin Astley, Simon Kirsopp, Stephen Carruthers, Natalie Mortimer, Simon Johnson and Dale Howey for the energetic, entertaining and supportive environment that makes going to work a pleasure.

Thanks to my course mates, 19 years later and I still enjoy bumping into you all today. I will carry those memories for a lifetime.

Thanks to Martin McConnell for standing by me when it was far easier not to, to every firefighter and junior officer on Bravo Red Watch, Charlie Red Watch and those on neighbouring stations who helped and supported me - I loved my detachments and the fantastic characters I got to work with. Thanks to Karen Soady, everyone in the Prevention and Education team and Terry Ray and the White Watch at Alpha who immediately accepted me as one of their own.

Thanks also to Louise Clarkson and Lynsey McVay for their support and advice. Their willingness to break barriers and improve conditions for others has helped shaped our fire service for the better.

Finally, thanks to Chris Lowther for his readiness to listen and find solutions and for inspiring an optimistic and inclusive future for Tyne and Wear Fire and Rescue Service.

About the Author

Kate lives in the North East of England and has been a firefighter for over 19 years. *Lifting the Fire Hydrant Lid* is her first book, written to reveal the difficulties faced by all firefighters, the additional tribulations of the female contingent and the true nature of their vocation. Born in County Durham, the second of four children and sandwiched between two brothers, Kate soon became accustomed to holding her own amongst male counterparts. After graduating from the University of Sunderland with a Sport Science degree, Kate was undecided as to her future career, but a chance visit to a Fire Service Training Centre changed her life forever. No stranger to challenging situations, Kate has climbed Mount Kilimanjaro and more recently adopted two boys as a single parent. Kate now works as a Breathing Apparatus Instructor at Tyne and Wear Fire and Rescue Training Centre.